Shalom, Jack

A CELEBRATION OF THE LIFE OF SGT JACOB ('JACK') GOLDSTEIN, RAFVR, 166 SQUADRON BOMBER COMMAND, KILLED IN ACTION 16 MARCH 1945

COMPILED AND EDITED BY JACK'S SON,
MICHAEL GOLDSTEIN CBE

Shalom, Jack

SHALOM, JACK

***

All rights reserved. No part of this publication may be reproduced, stored in a retrieval system, or transmitted, in any form, or by any means, electronic, mechanical, photocopying, recording or otherwise, without the prior permission in writing of the publishers TwigBooks.

© Michael Goldstein 2018

The right of **Michael Goldstein** to be identified as author and editor of this work had been asserted by him in accordance with the Copyright, Designs and Patent Act 1988.

Compiled & Edited with the assistance of Terry Gasking.

The views expressed in the text are those of the author and editor and should not be taken as representing those of any other person, institute, or organisation.

First published in 2018
ISBN 978-1-907953-70-5

Available from
Amazon, EBooks, Kindle

And leading book stores

SHALOM, JACK

CONTENTS

Introduction	4
Acknowledgements	6
Dedication	8
Polish Origins	9
Growing up in Bethnal Green	16
The Goldbergs	37
The Goldsteins' War Years	50
Jack the Airman	65
The last flight of RF154 ('TARFU')	78
After the Crash	90
Coping without Jack	100
The Others	112
Dürnbach	116
Kammerstein – Clarity at last	132
Remembering Jack	151
Reflections	155
Chronology	159
List of photographs and illustrations	162
References and Notes	169

SHALOM, JACK

INTRODUCTION

This book is about my father, Jacob Goldstein, known as 'Jack', who was killed in action as Mid-Upper Gunner in a Lancaster bomber on a raid over Nürnberg[1] on the night of 16 March 1945. It traces his family origins in Poland just before WW1, through his coming to England as a very young child and his early years as part of a large Jewish family in the East End of London, to his marriage and short life in the RAF Volunteer Reserve. It describes in detail the last hours and minutes of his life, his fate and final resting place, several stories of people in his life, and the profound effect he had on them.

Much of the text comprises eye-witness accounts and other personal recollections. This has been especially important to me, as I barely knew my father at all. I was not yet five-years-old when he was killed. Bringing all this information together in a coherent way and as comprehensively as I could, and working out what actually happened to him, has therefore been, literally, a revelation, and a hugely emotional experience for me. But I have written it with much wider intentions, because I hope the book will also be of value and pleasure to those with an interest in documentation by personal experiences of the horrors of war; the social history of the last hundred years; the positive side to immigration into the UK; the sacrifices made by thousands of incredibly brave people in Bomber Command; and more than all of these – the commitment and determination of ordinary people to fighting for peace and freedom, to create a better society for all.

There have already been several articles describing, in varying amounts of detail, the last flight of Jack's aircraft, Lancaster RF154.[2,3,4,5,6] All derive from the extensive research[7] carried out by my uncle, Ron Goldstein, my father's youngest brother, and my own posts to the BBC website WW2peopleswar based on this research.[8] But this is the first full and comprehensive account of Jack's life and death, incorporating and analysing more recent information about the crash and what followed.

Moreover, the book is not only about that traumatic and tragic night. I have tried to bring together much of what went before to provide a more complete biography – family, personal, and service-related – as well as describing the immediate aftermath and more recent events. In relation to family, I have drawn on three important sources. One is a Facebook site initiated by my cousin Naomi Yalin, dedicated to Meir and Malke Goldstein, Jack's paternal grandparents.[9] The second is a compilation of recollections of all the (then) surviving Goldstein siblings about their early lives. The book was entitled "And Then There Were Eleven," which referred to the (originally) eleven siblings in the family. The book was published privately in 1988 in loose-leaf format, but it sparked off various offshoots.[10] Finally, I need to make special mention of the collective autobiography[11] written by three of us: a Goldstein cousin, Susy Stone; Jack's youngest sister, Jean Lawrence; and me. My contribution included much directly about Jack, and both Susy and I gave views from the second generation of Goldsteins in the UK. But particularly relevant here is Jean's contribution, which gave a vivid picture of the childhood environment of the eleven Goldstein siblings growing up in Bethnal Green, where my grandparents Feigele ('Fanny') and Yosef ('Joseph') Goldstein had settled.

The book is written as from me, Jack's son. Because it is about people, I refer to all characters – my father and mother included – by their first names by which they were commonly known. Where applicable, I have used the Anglicised versions they used, except for Jack's parents, who hold a special place in this book, to emphasise their, and my, origin.[12]

I chose the title "*Shalom*, Jack" as derived from the simple entry '*Shalom!*' that my mother, Sadie, Jack's widow, poignantly wrote in the book of remembrance at the Dürnbach War Graves Cemetery where Jack is now buried, when I took her there for her first and only visit in 1979. This book is therefore a tribute to her as well as to Jack and the many thousands of others in Bomber Command who gave their lives for our freedom.

SHALOM, JACK

ACKNOWLEDGEMENTS

I have had great support for writing this book, and I wish to place on record my appreciation for all involved, particularly the sources I draw upon, as well as the help from my publisher, Twig Books.

I have tried to give due acknowledgment to all whom I have quoted or relied upon (references and notes are at the end of the book).

I am especially indebted to Jack's siblings, nearly all now sadly passed away, whose stories of their memories and lives up to the end of the Second World War[10] I have greatly relied upon in the early parts of this book.

I particularly wish to give my heartfelt thanks to my uncle Ron Goldstein, who provided so much of the base information about Jack's last flight that led to his death, painstakingly researched without the enormous benefits the developed internet now provides.[7] He has been a role model and an inspiration to me in so many ways; I could not possibly have conceived this book without his sense of purpose and contribution to my life. Underlying Ron's research was help afforded to him by several others – Jim Wright, Secretary of the 166 Squadron Association (now deceased); Mark Charnley, 166 Squadron Historian and Archivist; Martin Sugarman, Assistant Archivist of the Association of Jewish Ex-Servicemen and Women; three of Jack's fellow crew members: Alf White the Wireless Operator, 'Lefty' Etherington the Navigator, and especially Ted Hull the Flight Engineer (now deceased); and Dennis Hawley, an independent researcher supporting Martin Sugarman. I am myself obliged to Mark Charnley for some information used in this book.

I am forever grateful also to Ron's daughter, Marsha Rosenberg, who provided much background research data on the early histories of both the Goldstein family and my mother Sadie's family, the Goldbergs. My cousin Trevor Goldberg, son of my mother's eldest brother Ben, has also been of great help in providing information on our grandfather, Joe Goldberg.

SHALOM, JACK

I give my huge gratitude to Melanie Greiner (also using professionally her maiden name Herzog), a local historian living in Kammerstein, the village near which Jack's Lancaster bomber crashed, for bringing to my attention the detailed location and final moments of the crash, and for solving what for me were previously unresolved questions.

My sister, Leila Alleway, has for ever been a source of huge support and help – from teaching me to read and tell the time when I was three- or four-years old, to helping me get over the various challenges and disappointments in my life, and now to encouraging and guiding me on some of the facts described in this book.

My wife, Cyrrhian, has been wonderfully supportive (and tolerant!), and I cannot thank her enough for doing so very much to make this project happen, let alone for proofing and critiquing the text.

But, of course, the responsibility for this book is mine; I hope I have written and compiled it with accuracy and sensitivity, and that I have given due acknowledgement of others, but if I have in any way failed so to do, I apologise and trust that any offence will be understood as inadvertent.

Michael Goldstein
April 2018

SHALOM, JACK

DEDICATION

This book is primarily dedicated to the memory of my father, Sergeant Jacob ('Jack') Goldstein, Royal Air Force Volunteer Reserve 166 Squadron Bomber Command, service number 2235812, killed in action over Nürnberg, Germany in Lancaster bomber RF154 (AS-B) on 16 March 1945. In the words of the commemorative scroll issued to next-of-kin of those killed in World War 2, he is:

> *"held in honour as one who served King and Country in the world war of 1939-1945 and gave his life to save mankind from tyranny. May his sacrifice help to bring the peace and freedom for which he died."*

It is also in memory of my dear mother, Sadie, who passed away on 7 January 2001, still grieving for her beloved Jack; she devoted herself to ensuring her children had a better life, despite my sister Leila and me losing our father at so young an age.

And to the 57,871 airwomen, airmen and support personnel who died while serving Bomber Command, and their dependents, I offer this book.

Proceeds from sales of this book will be gifted to the Royal Air Force Benevolent Fund, which gave personal financial support to enable me to enter Hackney Downs Grammar School in 1950; and to the British Legion, which my family has supported for many years, and which does so much to ensure our fallen servicemen are forever remembered.

SHALOM, JACK

POLISH ORIGINS[13]

Jewish people have been a significant part of Poland's population since the 11th Century, finding it to be more accepting of them than elsewhere. They thrived and prospered for hundreds of years and were able to practise their religion. By the year 1500 there were 25,000 Jews in Poland; by 1578 this had grown to 100,000; by 1676 to 300,000; and by the end of the 18th Century there were about one million – some 12% of the population. But a series of wars, involving Ukraine, Russia and Sweden led to decline. Jews were isolated, displaced, crushingly taxed, banned from some occupations and education, demeaned and persecuted. They were confined to conditions of extreme poverty; blamed for the assassination of Czar Alexander II, which inspired a bloodbath of the Jewish population. A Russian government minister declared the hope "that one-third of the Jews would convert, one-third die, and one-third flee the country". And flee they did, as the looting, rape and massacres gathered strength. Every fresh organised massacre of Jews, the pogroms, triggered further emigration. Without hope, without help, the mass exodus to the West began.

It is with this background that we begin to trace Jack's origins. The village of Radzymin[14] [15] lies about 15 miles north of Warsaw. It is recorded since the beginning of the 15th century and was granted municipal rights in 1475. Jews started to settle there in the 17th century. By 1850 there were 1,278 Jews living in Radzymin, some 70% of the population, including a married couple named Meir and Malke Goldsztejn [Goldstein]. Their marriage had been arranged by their parents, as was the norm, to the extent that only when the groom raised his bride's veil did the young couple see each other for the first time. Malke earned a living delivering milk to the farming community, a yoke across her back. She contracted cholera as a young woman, losing much of her hair; consequently, she wore a *shetel* [wig] – not for religious tradition reasons.[16] Meir was devoutly religious, and earned meagre amounts from teaching Hebrew, supplemented by delivering coal in winter. It was an extremely hard life by today's standards, but they were thrifty and hard-working, and in due course saved enough money to buy a horse and cart to ease the pain of deliveries. But on the very day they took possession, the horse broke a leg and had to be destroyed! Life was never going to be easy.

Meir and Malke had five children that survived: three boys – Hershel, Yancze[17] and Yosef; and two girls – Rivka and Ruchze. They grew up in a background of poverty, repression and persecution, but within a loving family and caring community.

1 - Meir Goldstein and his wife Malke (with granddaughter Fay, daughter of Yancze and Choomah)

All young Jewish boys faced enforced conscription for up to 25 years into the Russian army. Yancze was the first to be conscripted and was sent to the Manchurian front during the imminence of the Russo-Japanese war (1904-05) where he suffered a serious knee injury, leading to him being discharged. Yosef was also conscripted, but he avoided active service by taking advantage of a stroke of good fortune. With slight tailoring experience he volunteered when his commanding officer needed some work done; he then spent a whole night unpicking the CO's uniform, made a pattern from it, put the uniform back together again, and produced a satisfactory new garment. He thus became tailor to officers, a safe and comfortable job until the end of his army career.

Unrest amongst the Jewish population grew out of fear of further repression, and groups of intellectuals and students began to emerge, seeking change. When Czar Nicholas II acceded to the

SHALOM, JACK

Russian throne in 1894, he began to repress these groups. This led to further fear and moves to emigration.

The children of Meir and Malke had grown up by the beginning of the 20th Century, and were marrying, settling down and moving to Warsaw. The eldest daughter, Rivka, married a Jacob Szmidek (also written as Scmideks[18]), a smart, shrewd man who was to become the family's successful and wealthy businessman known as 'Uncle Smith.' In 1902, Yosef married Feigele Kamen, a young dressmaker who left her family home because she was badly treated by her stepfather.

Every Jewish family in Warsaw was considering fleeing the oppressive and increasingly threatening regime. The issues were where, when, with whom, and how to finance the move. Jacob Szmidek took the plunge. He was enterprising and ambitious, frustrated by the restrictions on Jews, and aware of the constant danger to life and property. He had heard that tailors were in demand in London, due to the increased need for making uniforms for British soldiers fighting in South Africa (the Boer War began in 1899). So despite the wrench from his family, off he went, alone. When he arrived in England, an immigration officer decided that as the name Szmidek (or Scmideks[18]) was too difficult to spell, let alone pronounce, he would be called 'Smith', the name by which he was known for the rest of his life.

So 'Smith' became one of the thousands of Jews working long hours for little pay in the tailoring sweatshops of the impoverished East End of London. His wife, Rivka, joined him with their then two children, Sidney and Annie; Sylvia was born in London. Rivka soon became homesick, but Smith would not go back without sufficient money to start his own business in Poland. It took six years of hard work after arriving in London to be able to do that. And so, in 1906 the Smith family returned to Poland, buying a tailoring business – three shops and a workroom with accommodation above.

While the Smith business prospered, there was no end to persecution of Jews in Poland, and with the real threat of war in Europe Jews hastily began scattering all over the free world – between 1884 and 1903, over 500,000 Jewish emigrants from

SHALOM, JACK

Russia and Poland had fled to the United States; by 1907, a further 410,000. Thousands more had gone to Britain and elsewhere. Smith decided the time had come to leave Poland for good, this time with sufficient capital to start up his own business in London. He persuaded his brother-in-law, Yosef, whom he regarded as a hard-working, conscientious, clever man, to join him. He would stay with the Smith family in Leman Street, Whitechapel, and send for Feigele and her three children (Annie, Levy,[19] Jacob) when circumstances allowed.

The parting of Yosef from Feigele was tearful. She accepted the need to leave Poland and start a new life in a more benign environment, but she was reluctant for Yosef to leave her and the children behind. She was a clever dressmaker and able to support her children financially, but discovering she was pregnant with a fourth child, and convinced that war was coming, she soon decided she could wait no longer. She began to sell her possessions, parting even with her precious sewing machine and furniture. She could only take essentials – and that included her silver candlesticks, carefully wrapped in a tablecloth, which continued to be a feature of the Goldstein religious life when in England. There was no room for clothes for the new baby – God would provide.

In an advanced state of pregnancy, Feigele Goldstein left the apartment in Warsaw with her three young children and embarked on the long and arduous journey to England; the youngest child, Jack, was only 17 months old; Annie was five, and Levy[19] (later known as Lou) just four. She could speak no English, and in case the expected child was born en route, she bought a first-class train ticket to Vienna, where she had to wait for visas. When her money ran out, she had to cable her shocked husband for money to continue the journey – a journey he had no idea until that moment she was undertaking! Yosef could not afford to send Feigele the money, but Smith came to the rescue. And it was Smith who provided the rent for the Goldstein's first home in England, rented rooms in 59 Lambeth Street in the docks area of East London.

The Goldstein's fourth child, their first British child, Esther, was born just a few days after Feigele arrived in England, on 20 November 1913. The nurses from The London Hospital who came for the delivery at the family home brought with them baby clothes at the request of Yosef, as he had no time to provide them himself.

2 - Feigele and Yosef in 1914 with children (left to right) Jack, Esther, Annie, and Lou

In due course, the Goldstein family grew to eleven children:[19]

- **Annie**
  1908 – 1976
  Married Solly Leboff, 1927.
  Children: Nita (1928) and Leon (1933).

- Leib or Levy; formally changed name (1947) from Leib Goldstein to Louis Grayson; known as **Lou**
  1909 - 1961
  Married Esther Levy, 1938.
  Children: Sandra (1940) and Brian (1942).

- Jacob; known as **Jack**
  1912 - 1945
  Married Sarah Goldberg (known as Sadie), 1934.
  Children: Leila (1934) and Michael (1939).

SHALOM, JACK

- **Esther**
  1913 - 2011
  Married Jack Rosenquit, 1936.
  Children: Laurence (1939) and Martin (1941) (Rosen).

- **Gertie**
  1916 - 2018
  Married Alf Denenberg, 1938.
  Children: Margaret (1941), Peter (1946), and Stephen (1947).

- Morris; changed family surname towards 1948 to Gordon; known as **Mossy**
  1916 – 2001
  Married Nita Stern, 1940.
  Children: Roy (1941), Marilyn (1948), Sharon (1948), and Helen (1955).

- Polly or Pauline;[19][20] known as **Polly**
  1918 - 2008
  Married Mendel (known as Wolfie) Kalicstein,[20] 27 February 1951; changed family surname to Kail after 1954.
  Children: Paul (1943), Julie (1952), and Libby (1954).

- Myer or Michael Meyer; known as **Mick**
  1920 - 2005
  Married Sylvia Goldstein (daughter of Yancze[17]), 1946.
  Children: Naomi (1949) and Susan (known as Susy) (1952).

- Debbie or Deborah; known as **Debbie**
  1921 - 2005
  Married Alec Lubdofsky (later, Davis), 1941.
  Child: Barry (1942).

- Reuben or Ronald; known as Ronnie or **Ron**
  1923 -
  Married Nita Schneiderman, 1949.
  Children: Marsha (1951) and Ruth (1955).

- **Jean**
  1929 – 2016
  Married Leslie Lawrence, 1952.
  Children: Nicola (1958) and Jonathan (1961).

The flight of the Goldsteins from Radzymin was not only sensible and timely, but was also wise in the longer term.[14][15] When German troops entered Radzymin at the outbreak of WW2 in September 1939, there were about 3,900 Jewish inhabitants. A year later, the Nazis created a ghetto in the town, incarcerating Jews from Radzymin and others displaced from nearby localities. Many died from famine, executions, typhus and other diseases. On 3 October 1942, all Jews surviving in the Radzymin ghetto, around 2,500, were sent to the extermination camp in Treblinka. Only 40 survived the Holocaust. The Jewish cemetery in Radzymin, which had been opened in the 18th century was devastated by the Germans during the war. Not even one gravestone remained. At present, the former cemetery is a park; there is a concrete plinth with a marble commemorative plaque to *Tzaddik*-Jakow Arie Guterman,[21] one of the founders of the Hasidic movement, who lived in Radzymin.

SHALOM, JACK

GROWING UP IN BETHNAL GREEN[22] [23]

After a couple of years working for others, Yosef decided it was time he worked for himself. In any case, they needed a larger home, and more income, to cater for their growing number of children. They settled near the docks where they had first arrived in England, at 21 Boreham Street, where he could also set up his own workshop.[24] The area had previously been occupied by Huguenot refugees fleeing from oppression in France, hence some of the streets were named after French cities such as Navarre Street and Rochelle Street. It was at 21 Boreham Street where in due time Mossy, Gertie, Mick, Debbie, Ron and Jean were born.

3 - Houses in Boreham Street, Bethnal Green, London

The area was characterised by poverty and overcrowding, many living in the 27,000 tenement blocks (compared with 11,000 ordinary houses). Bethnal Green had a high proportion, 44.6 per cent, of poor and very poor (44.6 per cent in the 1880s), mostly casual labourers and people under-employed in the furniture and dress trades.[25]

Everyone in the area knew Boreham Street. It comprised 24 redbrick houses, 4-stories high, 12 on each side of the street. Number 21 was the fourth house from the southerly end, on the west side of the street. The top floors of every house were used as workshops for the families' trades – tailors and furriers in the main.

Nearby were many properties occupied by Jewish cabinet makers and upholsterers. Each of the houses was occupied by one or more Jewish families, so Boreham Street was known locally as 'Jews Alley.' It was a cul-de-sac and traffic-free, so provided a safe area for the children to play – with skipping, hoops, hopscotch, 'gimmy-gimmy-nacks',[26] 'statues', diablo, flicking cigarette cards, swinging from ropes attached to the lamp-posts at the ends of the street, football, cricket and other ball-games. The boys made scooters from planks of wood and roller bearings, which they used to get around, for example for adventures in Victoria Park.

At *Pesach* [Passover], the street was a magnet for Jewish children across the entire neighbourhood. Hazelnuts were the currency for all kinds of games – such as pitching nuts onto a coin or into a small hole in a box; or rolling nuts into a small circle with the winner taking the 'kitty.' There were perhaps 100 or more 'pitches' of children setting up the various games.

In summer evenings, the parents would relax on chairs outside their doors, sharing cold drinks and gossip, and idly watching their children play. Sometimes the children were sent to buy the hot salt-beef sandwiches from Simons in Bethnal Green Road or take an empty jug to be filled with cream soda and ice-cream from Reubens, the confectioners around the corner.

Running parallel to Boreham Street and accessed by a small alleyway at the northern end, was Brick Lane. This still famous market sold everything imaginable – fresh food, homeware, clothing, furniture. There were lovely smells of herrings, pickled cucumbers and fresh brown bread, and at the end of the market some not-so-lovely smells… The market also provided for the poorer locals – children with holes in their hand-me-down clothes and threadbare shoes would wait for vegetables and fruit to be thrown away at the end of the day and take their spoils home for their families to share.

The children of Boreham Street were in and out of each other's houses. The families were all mutually supportive, helping each other out in times of need. The Goldstein family regularly provided food for the Sabbath to the Allsuch family across the road at number four - a pan of soup, a tray of fried or *gefilte* fish,[27] some fresh *strudel;*[28] Mr Allsuch was a chronic invalid since being gassed in WW1, and his wife had him to nurse while bringing up their five children. Yosef himself was well-known to be generous, unable to decline a request for help. He would always guarantee a bank loan for a neighbour needing money urgently for whatever reason. 'It's a *mitzva* [God's commandment] to help our neighbours,' he would say, to which Feigele cried '*Gevalt!* [help!]' knowing that if the neighbour defaulted on the repayment, Yosef would make good the bank loan. On one occasion he was declared bankrupt through helping a friend. The attitude of helping fellow human beings, whatever the circumstances was a good lesson for the children. Gertie's route to secondary school took her underneath the Wheeler Street railway arches, where down-and-outs made their home; she was known to give them some of her lunch money and have less for herself.

At the end of Boreham Street was Peter Street.[29] The junction between the two streets was a social divide, because just as only Jews lived in Boreham Street, so Peter Street was made up entirely of Christian families. The children from both streets mixed well at school, but not at home. Parents told their Jewish children not to make a noise outside the nearby church or when going into Christian areas – no doubt derived from their memories and images of bad treatment at the hands of Polish Christians.

Feigele accepted the growing family, saying, in Yiddish, "*Gott vill ferzorgen*" [God will provide], while for Yosef "the more children we have, the harder I will have to work, the more money I will make." And work hard he did. From dawn to dusk, the master-tailor laboured in the workshop at the top of the house. He was exceptionally skilful at manipulating patterns to save on cloth. He thus maximised the cloth left over from the rolls provided by the firms for which he made garments (coats and suits), thus accumulating 'cabbage', as it was called, to make more garments he sold privately or to tally-men,[30] thus supplementing his income. He was also able to make clothes for the children at no cost; they were thus always well dressed for the Jewish holidays.

During WW1, when threatened Zeppelin bombings caused masses of frightened families to get out of London, the sisters-in-law,

SHALOM, JACK

Feigele and Rivka, and their children, evacuated to Burgess Hill, Sussex, near to Wivelsfield Station, living in non-Jewish homes. The husbands, Yosef and Smith, stayed in London to work during the week but travelled to Burgess Hill at weekends to be with their families. Polly was born in Burgess Hill, perhaps contributing to her love of the country in later life, and why she joined the Women's Land Army in WW2.

With so many occupants and functions, Number 21 Boreham Street had to be well organised. The front doorstep was kept scrubbed clean and whitened with hearthstone, and the brass letterbox kept well-shined. A string dangling through the letterbox and attached to the lock enabled the children to get in without having to have a key – no concerns about burglars! The two rooms on the ground floor were bedrooms for the siblings, one for the girls and one for the boys, although when babies they would sleep in the parents' bedroom. At the rear end of the passageway between the two bedrooms was the wash-house with its large copper, and a door leading to the tiny backyard and outside toilet. On the first floor was the kitchen, with a sink on the landing for washing (in ice-cold water), and a humble but clean toilet, shared by everyone including the people working in the top-floor workshop. 'Toilet paper' was torn-up newspaper squares, hung on a nail by a loop of coarse string. On the first floor was also the 'front room' – the lounge and living room, where the family could relax and play - with its crystal chandelier, brown leather sofa, heavy mahogany furniture, and shiny black-lacquered HMV gramophone. This was the place for entertaining visitors such as boyfriends and girlfriends; it was also the place for special occasions such as the Passover meals. On the next floor was the bedroom of Feigele and Yosef, and the cutting-room-cum-office for the business. This latter room also served to store cloth and completed garments which did not remain there for long as they needed to be converted to income – most were promptly delivered in barrows hired for 6d (2½p) a day from around the corner. Finally, at the very top of the house was the large attic workshop, with its sloping roof, benches, long trestles, machines, and black outsize flat-irons on dirty white ironing cloths; piles of fabrics, in various stages of cutting and sewing, and remnants galore, were strewn all around. The younger children were forbidden to climb the steep, rough wooden stairs to the workshop, which therefore generated both a fear and a fascination.

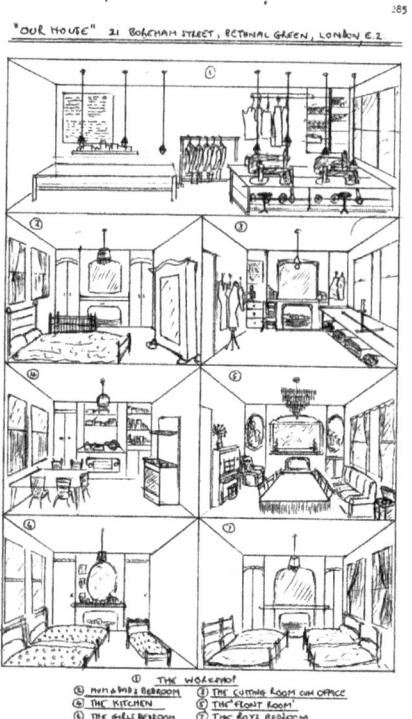

4 - Ron Goldstein's sketch of the layout of 21 Boreham Street

Number 21 Boreham Street was basic – originally gas-lit; no bathroom; an outside toilet; no running hot water; clothes scrubbed on a washboard with hard yellow soap; a hand-powered mangle; masses of ironing using a heavy press-iron heated on the stove. The smaller children were bathed one-by-one in a zinc bath on the kitchen floor in front of the stove, with water brought laboriously in from the sink on the landing and heated on the stove in kettles and pots; older children, and their parents, making do with a weekly visit to the public baths.

But through sheer hard work and commitment to the children, the house of Feigele and Yosef Goldstein was the first in the street to have electricity, and they were the first to run a car (a Morris Oxford). They could even afford two (non-Jewish) live-in housemaids, sisters Alice and Edie Harrison, who slept in the same room as the Goldstein girls. They were each paid £1 a week, significantly above the going rate, in addition to their board and keep. For Feigele, it was only right to treat them well, but she also did it to reduce the likelihood of them 'helping themselves.' Alice and Edie sometimes took a few of the young Goldsteins for a day trip to their family home at Laindon in the Essex countryside – a great treat for the East End kids, with unheard-of freedoms and experiences. They stayed with the Goldsteins for years, until they were married, becoming almost part of the family.

It was gruelling work for Feigele, on top of the strain of repeated child-bearing. Even with two housemaids, Feigele did all the shopping and cooking – a stone (6.4kg) of fish from Bethnal Green Market to be fried in oil; three chickens from Sarah the butcher to pluck for the Sabbath meal; a stone of potatoes to peel every day.... She was a real dynamo and did all she could on a meagre allowance to ensure her children were as well fed as possible – using no additives and good, wholesome ingredients to keep the family in good health. No wonder Feigele had to have a one-hour nap every day to get through it all!

Feigele was an accomplished cook, and each week made large numbers of cakes and *kichlach*[31] laid out on big trays. The family stove was not large enough to take them, but Kossoff's, the bakers around the corner, baked them in their great ovens for 1d [one penny in pre-decimal currency – about 0.004p in today's money], ready for collection on Friday afternoons by the children taking turns. Often, a large casserole of *cholent*[32] was also taken for the Sabbath lunch.

Meals came in relays. Lunch was at 11.30am for the youngest, and at noon for those coming home from school to eat. At 1pm, Yosef and the two oldest boys, Lou and Jack, would take a quick break from the workshop to snatch a bite to eat – and study form for a bet on the horses or dogs; gambling was an important part of the Goldstein household.

Sleeping arrangements were even more of a challenge. The little ones slept two, three, and sometimes four in a bed *zu feesens* [feet-to-feet] with two at each end. Bed-time was when some of the children's greatest fun took place. One game was to play 'conjours', in which they balanced on their heads on the pillows while climbing with their feet up the wall. Feigele despaired at the damage to the flowered wallpaper, already marked by squashed bed-bugs – another of their night-time activities being the impossible task of ridding the beds of these frightening creatures.

In the evening, Feigele and Yosef would either walk out together, dressed in their best clothes, or Feigele would prepare salt-beef sandwiches for the night-time solo-whist parties – one of Yosef's enduring pleasures.

Yosef taught himself to read and write English, aided by reading the dog- and horse-racing columns of the newspapers. He insisted this was the language of the household – Yiddish was only for things they wanted to keep from the children, although Feigele frequently lapsed into Yiddish.

The Smiths, the 'rich' relations, soon moved out of the East End to the then smart area of Stamford Hill, and later to Golders Green, then a semi-rural location. Uncle Smith remained a big figure in the family, doing business with Yosef and coming back to Boreham Street for all-night games of solo-whist.

The homes the Smiths created were full of luxury of the times – lacquered furniture, carpets, crystal, silver; a bathroom with running hot water; a chauffeur-driven car; a cook-housekeeper…. This was a huge contrast to 21 Boreham Street…black beetles from the tannery in the backyard; bedbugs and hair lice which plagued the whole neighbourhood, making fumigation and delousing a regular necessity; rats occasionally finding their way into the workshop. Jean's descriptions of these horrors were written so eloquently and with feeling, that they warrant recording here:[10] [11]

> "I was seven years old. I sat in the classroom which gave off the hall, and where the dark brown of the tiles covering the lower part of the walls was mixed with mottling of cream and shone, all glazed. There was normally a feeling of comfort inside me, in this room, from the companionable movement of the other children and the warm, regulated ambience, but today I kept glancing towards the door.

Finally, she came, as I knew she would, the nurse, dark blue and white in uniform, the white starched and with her face with its very white skin and mauvish lips, very straight. She had a paper in her hand which she lifted carefully and read from in such a clear, firm fashion. She read the list of children who were to go and have their hair de-nitted, de-loused – the ones who had been discovered when - half an hour ago – she had inspected their heads, with the long precise strokes of her oblong metal comb, which flicked the hair back to reveal the parting along which the creatures could clearly be seen. My name was there, of course, and obediently and numb, anaesthetized, hardly conscious of moving across the half-room, I went to line up with the others. The group of children thus assembled at the door, looking up at the nurse occasionally, did not look at each other, not out of shame, just that there was no point in such communication. The act of going was the overwhelming thing, and we shuffled away, to the place with the soft soap whose smell bit into your nostrils, not entirely unpleasant but just very different and strong. My sense of smell was never very fine, but this scent, with the gooey texture of the soap, olive green, and translucently liquid, affected me. The place was tiled, too, but unlike those in the classroom these squares held no colour or warmth. Later when I knew the word I would have called them 'functional': that is all they were, blending with the grey, finely-veined sink over which I bent my hair, for cleansing.

The trouble with the whole process was that I could never satisfy them. I would be temporarily clean, but the nits and lice would return, and it would all happen again, so that it was not an experience with any start or finish. It was part of a pattern which was to recur, like living in the midst of a roll of patterned wallpaper.

At home, in the small, square bedroom where my bed touched that of my parents, I would sit combing for nits with the square metal comb, looking and finding, cracking them with my thumbnails and crushing with the flat of the nail the occasional still or slowly-moving louse, which left its almost colourless smear along the comb. Gradually the nits grew fewer and fewer until the search was futile and complete. It was not bad when it was over: there was a satisfaction there."

"The bugs, the beetles [and the baths] were all important, in their own way. The bugs were a strictly bedroom phenomenon, very occasionally seen settled on a wall, but almost always in bed. It seemed slightly odd, since there were so many of them, that they were not to be seen on the top of the over-bed, the down-filled half-fluffy, half-lumpy quilt-like, sheet-shrouded eiderdown which kept you very warm at night. Perhaps they too preferred to burrow in the warmth of the inside of the coverings, and might die on top: for whatever reason, they lay concealed for the most part inside, in the folds and it was constantly a matter for surprise to find one suddenly appearing, moving or still, against the starched whiteness of the sheeting.

There were at least three types of bug, first the mature, dark brownish-red adult, large enough for the slight ridging to appear on his shiny carapace, shield-like in shape, with legs too small to see. His junior version was half the size and twice as red, crimson, obviously young, while the baby had a translucence about its creamy, red-edged flesh. Crack the bug and the blood – if blood it was – it looked like blood – spilt and smeared the bed. Not pleasant, but better than a creeping creature, or even a still one, there all the time, to startle you horridly, and to crawl.

The beetles were not mine, like the bugs, who belonged in the family mattresses and presumably in the walls. The beetles belonged to the leather factory whose wall was the same wall which edged our yard, and whose hooter calling the never-see work-force woke me sleeping in my parents' bedroom. Not surprising after all that the beetles flouted observance of the boundary wall and made free with the yard, traversing the oblong with impunity - or did my brothers kill them? - I never thought of that - and presenting a problem. The problem would not have existed but that the

> lavatory with its newspaper squares on the nail was actually in the yard, and to use it meant crossing the yard and risking the sight of the beetles, hardly habituate to, pressed hard in their long oval against the wall, or stationary, exposed on the yard, or making a jerky way across it."

But despite these horrors, the children grew up in a deeply loving and hugely caring environment. As Gertie wrote so poignantly in 1991:[23]

> "We grew up in the slums of the East End, but we were not slum children, because our parents did not have a slum mentality.
> They taught us to be independent, self-reliant and industrious. They gave us not riches, but something much more valuable, a sense of our own worth.
> We were never bored, never lonely, never alone. We, who were eleven are now eight, all over retirement age, and still as close as we were as children.
> We are rarely bored. We write, we paint, we love life, and we still swim!"

Yosef and Feigele were always boasting about their family: *"the sheinster fun aller kinder"* [the most beautiful of all children]. The siblings played together and shared experiences of Brownies, Girl Guides, Scouts, The Jewish Lads Brigade, The Boys Brigade, the Cambridge and Bethnal Green Boys' Club,[33] Hebrew classes, and later, Zionist groups. Any discord was soon settled by diplomatic Feigele, with soothing words in Yiddish – *"Shush, Kinder"* [Quiet children], *"Shrei nicht"*, [Don't shout], *"Kim shoin"* [Get a move on], *"Gay to school, geshvint"* [Go to school, quickly]. If all that failed, the matter was resolved by the stern message of Yosef's flashing eyes and his thundering voice – never any physical chastisement.

All the children went to Rochelle Street Elementary School. It was non-denominational, but as nearly all the pupils were Jewish (around 90% spoke Yiddish) school finished early on Fridays for the Sabbath, and on Jewish holy days. The pupils were from refugee families from all over the world; a real mix of colour, creed and culture, but all with the same backgrounds of families struggling to survive and succeed. There was no obesity, rather hunger, shoelessness and poverty. Discipline was strict, with use of the cane by the Headteacher, swiped across the out-stretched palm of the hand, the normal method of punishment to ensure children behaved and kept to the rules. Feigele was well-known to the staff, supporting her children in everything they did through thick and thin – and often fighting their corners. Many a half-penny pocket money was spent with Campbell, the toffee-man on his converted tricycle outside the school, and the glorious ice-creams from the 'Hokey-Pokey, Penny-a-Lump' man with his cart in Peter Street.

5 - From left to right: Ronnie, Debby, Mick, and Polly

6 - With friends: Polly far left; Mick with cap; Ron front row left; Debby far right

They loved the trips to the countryside on which their parents were sometimes able to take them. Mossy recalled[10] one occasion when Yosef hired a pony and trap for such a trip. "Once we left smoky old London the air was sweet. The clip-clop of the pony's hooves, the sheer joy of the country scene, and the picnic that followed, created a love for the open air." The family also enjoyed days on the River Thames at Richmond - buying ice-cream and strawberries from passing boats, returning home at dusk, tired and happy. They were fortunate to be able to go on month-long summer holidays to a farm in Goff's Oak, Cheshunt, together with the children of one of

Yosef's customers, Mr Clow; such wonderful experiences and happy times for them.

They were all mad about swimming, regularly going to nearby York Hall Baths in Old Ford Road (now a health and leisure centre) and Haggerston Baths in Whiston Road (now awaiting redevelopment), or, on summer weekends, the open-air pool in Victoria Park. They were all good swimmers. One year four of the girls swam for the Bethnal Green Jewish Girls Club. To Feigele's joy, and the crowd's amusement, the tannoy announced the winners of the team event: "E. Goldstein, G. Goldstein, P. Goldstein and D. Goldstein" – Esther, Gertie, Polly and Debbie.

7 - Polly in swim-suit

The children were brought up religiously but not strictly *frum*,[34] with generally kosher food, worship in Bethnal Green Great Synagogue, particularly on Jewish holy days. The boys all went there for after-school *cheder*[35] on Monday to Thursday 5-8pm, and 10am-1pm on Sunday. The girls also had evening Hebrew classes at Rochelle Street School.

The girls particularly became very much involved with the Arts. Libraries were all important, as they could not afford a regular supply of books of their own. Bethnal Green and Whitechapel Libraries were important parts of their out-of-school education and became the only quiet places available for homework to be done, even though it was a good walk away from Boreham Street. Esther became an accomplished pianist, thanks to private lessons; she was an active player with the Old Stepnians Amateur Operatic Society, especially performing in Gilbert and Sullivan operas. Gertie had a passion for literature, joining the literature appreciation class at Toynbee Hall, and falling in love with the works of Rupert Brooke; she was writing poetry and prose from her school years. Ron learned to play the harmonica and formed a group with three friends called 'The Four Harmonica Kids,' which won a talent competition at the Mile End Empire and performed at weddings etc. They broke up when they began to get jobs and could not find the time for practice.

As teenagers and beyond, the Goldsteins became very much involved in politics and social activism. They went to lectures at Toynbee Hall, and to the Workers' Circle for talks and debates on current political affairs, as well as concerts. With the coming of the General Strike in 1926 and the economic problems of the times, with massive unemployment and growing depravation, it was little wonder that the Jewish youth turned to the Left, to the Labour League of Youth and the Young Communists. Fascism began to grow in the East End – racists, anti-Semites, Nazi-supporters and hooligans under the leadership of Sir Oswald Moseley and his British Union of Fascists. It attracted youngsters who were angry at the unemployment and poverty around them. The fascists offered uniforms (the Blackshirts) and opportunity to vent their repressed emotions. The Jewish community was the object of their attention. The Communist Party seemed to some to be the only people attempting to fight them, as well as standing up for quality of life for all. The Young Communist League in Aldgate recruited many from the Jewish youth in the area, including Gertie and Polly. They were on dangerous grounds at times – whitewashing walls with anti-fascist and anti-war slogans; heckling at fascist rallies; marching and shouting through the streets, sometimes ending in fights. Later, they became disillusioned, realising they had been duped into believing they had joined a mildly-innocent youth club with socialist tendencies rather than the hard-left extremist party.

The British Union of Fascists organised marches through the streets, often in predominantly Jewish areas. One such march in London's East End on 4 October 1936, which became known as 'The Battle of Cable Street,' was responded to by thousands from the local Jewish population, including some of the Goldsteins, well supported by the dockers. Feigele, clutching a handkerchief to her mouth, petrified as her children left the house with banners and much courage to join those trying to stop the Moseley march, cried: "Be careful. For God's sake, be careful!" Six-year-old Jean crouched, frightened, under a table. Ron, aged 13, was forbidden from going by Feigele and Yosef. The uprising of the Jews, dockers and others stopped the fascists at Gardiner's Corner, Aldgate with the cry "They shall not pass!" Mounted police with truncheons broke up the fighting and many were hurt, but the march failed. As evening fell, the Goldstein siblings limped home, exhausted, dishevelled, some bruised and scratched, but feeling so good they had done their bit to stop the fascists. There, at the front door, was Feigele, waiting with a mixture of English and Yiddish "T'ank *Gott*, t'ank *Gott*!", hot soup, warm water, cotton wool and disinfectant.

Yosef's business was always a struggle – and seasonal. In the busy period, he and the older brothers worked all hours God sent, sometimes from as early as 4am until midnight. Mossy recalls[10] one occasion when he was slogging away at a sewing machine at 11.30pm to complete an order, appealing to God; "Surely this is not to be my fate for the rest of my working life?" But in the inevitable slack times there was no work, no income; no welfare payments or benefits then! Feigele had to rely on credit to feed and clothe her brood, running up debts of £100 or more – a fortune in this days. Pawnbrokers thrived, not on valuables, for there were precious few of those, but on everyday needs – shoes, blankets, the Sabbath suit, candlesticks – anything that could be pawned on Monday until pay-day on Friday. And when the Depression hit the country, Yosef's business was even harder hit because it lasted longer than the normal slack periods. Sales of coats and costumes dried up; shopkeepers could not pay their bills, let alone order more stock. With little or no income, the family was in financial trouble; feeding eleven hungry children, including some very young ones (the youngest was Jean, born in 1929 at around the start of the Depression), was a real challenge. The strain caused some discord in the household as Feigele and Yosef argued about how to pay the butcher, the fishmonger, the intimidating tally-woman Sonya and others. What little money they had would not go far enough. Feigele wanted it all to pay the tradespeople who provided the food for the children, while Yosef felt he had to pay his workpeople first or they and their families would go hungry. It was not a happy time in number 21.

But not for long, as Yosef was an incurable optimist. Soon he found new customers and made fresh designs, providing sufficient to get by – give the tradespeople and Sonya enough to keep them happy until the general economy improved, and things got back to an even keel.

Feigele and Yosef had their health problems, as was inevitable with their demanding lifestyle, their environment, and limited healthcare at the time. In 1937, Feigele was smitten by glaucoma and had to have an eye removed; she wore a glass eye from then on. During Feigele's incapacitation, Debbie, just 16-years-old at the time, had to take over all the family cooking as the older girls had either married and left home, about to marry, and in any case were working. This was a huge undertaking for the young girl, as she had never had to do much cooking before.

Yosef was a keen gambler. He loved a flutter. There were no betting shops then, of course, and bookmakers were illegal, but the boys were taught how to place bets with local 'bookies' and how to post look-outs to avoid being caught by the police. Yosef was a clever card-player and enjoyed the regular card nights at home as well as trying his luck at the Whist Drive, often taking Feigele for the night out. When greyhound racing was introduced, he became an avid fan. He would spend all evening at the local track ('the dogs'), often taking the elder brothers. As long as Yosef won, Feigele didn't mind him gambling, not least because she got a share of the winnings and more money was available to spend on food and 'extras' for the children. But it was a different matter when he lost…

On one occasion, Yosef and sons Lou, Jack and Mossy were going to Wembley dog track in the family car. Jack had recently driven into a lamp-post, so Lou was driving. They were late, so Lou was driving "like a lunatic." Mossy regarded Lou as just as bad a driver as Jack, and indeed on the way he came near to running down a pedestrian, who was sent sprawling…. not hurt, fortunately, and amazingly apologetic rather than angry. Nevertheless, the journey was further delayed, and they just failed to place a bet on the dog that Yosef was certain was going to win – which it did, with not a penny of the Goldstein money placed on it!

Yosef was just as addicted to betting on horse-racing. He was sure that one day he would get that 'big win' which would solve all his money worries. That dream never came true, but there were more modest wins, giving joyous times for the household, bringing much-welcomed supplementary money for Feigele and all the children.

For both Feigele and Yosef, education of their children was paramount, even though they had no formal education themselves. Actually, Yosef had begun school in Poland, but the schoolmaster had told him to go away and not return until he put shoes on; as the family could not afford to buy shoes, he did not return. Two weeks of schooling was all he had, apart from a form of religious education.[11] But Feigele and Yosef both recognised the importance of education for their children, so they could have better lives than they had been able to enjoy. Their children were all "brilliant clever", as Feigele would say with pride, and they would do all they could to enable them to achieve their potential. But there were also restrictions. Thus, Esther (as did Jean and Gertie later) went to the Central Girls Foundation School in Spital Square, rather than taking up a Junior County Scholarship at the famous Greycoats School because it meant boarding – eating un-kosher food and growing away from *Yiddishkeit* [Jewish traditions]; and not taking her Piano Scholarship for the Royal School of Music because music was thought to be a world riddled with antisemitism. But Lou went to boarding school. Ron passed 'The Scholarship,' the 11+ examination which most children then took in their last year of primary school to determine which secondary educational stream they could enter (Grammar, Central or Secondary Modern).[36] He went to the local Grammar School, Parmiters, but was unhappy there. He was without his friends and considered the environment to be 'snobbish'. Moreover, he found that the homework set to be done every evening interfered with his Club and other social activities. So he played 'hookey' and forged absence notes from his parents. Inevitably he was found out, and before his father could take action he ran away from home. He got as far as Tower Bridge before deciding to turn back. He was allowed to leave Parmiters and transfer to Mansfield Street Central School; Mick, Polly and Debbie were already pupils there, having not managed to pass the 11+ examination.

Times were tough, and there were periods when continuing in education beyond the then compulsory age of 14 became too selfish a path to take; the teenagers had to help the family income by getting jobs. For example, in her last year at secondary school, Debbie won a scholarship to go to a trade school; she opted for photography at Bloomsbury Technical College, but at the last minute decided to go to work instead to help the family income, becoming, at the age of 14, an apprentice to a high-class dressmaker at 6/- (30p) a week.

Gertie also decided she had to leave school before Matriculation, to go out to work to help the family income; at a big City milliner, she earned 5/- (5 shillings, 25p) a week, but later moved to a shop in Bethnal Green working seven days a week (to 8pm on weekdays and 9pm on Saturdays) for £2, giving £1 to Feigele for her keep.

Polly had a strong artistic disposition, and often arranged some of the girls' hair at the Girls Club. She decided that was to be her career and having failed to get a trade scholarship in hairdressing settled for a job as an apprentice hairdresser before her 14th birthday, the start of her hairdressing career.

Mick won a scholarship to go to Regent Street Polytechnic (now the University of Westminster); he wanted to study architecture, but Yosef felt it essential for him to get a 'trade', so he went into ladies' and gents' hairdressing, massage, wig-making, and trichology (hair and scalp health). Although he was not too happy with the long hours on his feet all day, he agreed to join his sister Polly who was then opening a ladies' hairdressing salon. The business was not that successful, but in any case, Mick was shortly called up to the forces in the early months of WW2.

But getting jobs was sometimes problematic because anti-Semitism came in the way. Esther was determined to get a job in the City, but was not even granted an interview with the name Goldstein; only when she gave her name as 'Gordon' did she get a look-in. Having passed speed tests with flying colours, the answer 'Jewish' to the then-allowed question "Religion?" brought the invariable rejection response: "The position has now been filled." Sometime later, in another job, she discovered some colleagues using the firms' facilities to print virulently anti-Semitic literature for the British Union of Fascists. Undecided what to do, and deeply disturbed, she asked her father for advice. Yosef was unequivocal: "Anti-Semitism is a cancer, it must be rooted out. In Poland we ran away when the Cossacks beat us with sticks; but in England we can stand up for ourselves. Tell [your boss] what these wicked people are doing when they should be working." She did, to good effect.

For the boys it was hoped that they would go into the family business, and that is just what Lou and Jack did. Ron had a variety of jobs, initially hoping to make a career in Fleet Street, but then took a few jobs in the clothing business, finally joining the family firm as a machinist at the age of 16.

8 - Annie

9 - Esther

10 - Gertie

As the children grew older, their interests in the opposite sex grew too. Being with family and sharing interests with them was one thing. But fraternising with others became more dominant. The sisters would find opportunities to be around the boys from Cambridge and Bethnal Green Boys' Club, while the brothers kept their eyes on members of the Girls' Club. The Clubs were led by some Cambridge graduates and business people to provide a meeting place for the sons and daughters of Jewish immigrants, recognising the importance of developing them as strong British citizens. Their premises were at an old converted pub, The Blue Anchor, in Chance Street. As well as providing sport and fitness regimes, with teams competing in local competitions, there were opportunities in photography, art, drama, chess – and for discussion and debate about contemporary issues. Annual camping holidays in the country were a wonderful experience to develop camaraderie and to enjoy life outside the over-crowded areas where they lived. There is no doubt that the Clubs made a huge positive difference to the development of the members of the emerging society.

Ballroom and other dancing was also popular in clubs and dance-halls in the East End, such as the La Bohème in Whitechapel, which gave another opportunity to meet the opposite sex.

11 - Jack   **12 - Jean**

Near their Boreham Street home was a little park where the famous Shoreditch bandstand played one evening a week, surrounded by vendors selling sweets and the like to masses of exuberant teenagers giving each other 'the eye.' The little sweet shop in Brick Lane, owned by a family called Ginsberg and known as Ginty's, was another regular haunt for teenagers in the area – sharing views on politics, music and setting the world to right. Whitechapel High Street was the meeting place for the Jewish boys and girls of the East End after evening homework, especially at weekends; 'getting off' with the opposite sex was the desired outcome. But in any case, there were plenty of friends in Boreham Street itself, and their relatives and friends living nearby. At the age of 16, Esther began dating Jack Rosenquit,[37] a friend of Mick Miller who lived at number 15, and a few years later married him. Mossy met and later married Nita Stern, whom he met when he went on holiday with a few Club friends and they joined up with a party from the Girls Club. Gertie married Alf Denenberg who worked in the cleaners' shop opposite where she worked in Bethnal Green Road. Jean met Harold Pinter at Club, a young man who was destined to become a Nobel Prize-winning English playwright, screenwriter, director and actor, and one of the most influential modern British dramatists with a writing career spanning more than 50 years; she described him thus:[10] [11]

> "…a nice boy, a thoughtful cove who joined with me in relishing our books. He took me home, and round a lamp-post where Bouverie Road joined Manor Road, he twined himself, reciting 'Prufrock':[38] "I grow old… I grow old… I shall wear the bottoms of my trousers rolled." We were sixteen, and the words, and the moment had meaning. Harold borrowed from me two books: a complete Shakespeare and a Rupert Brooke, never to return!"

Lily Cohen from number 16 Boreham Street was girlfriend to Mick Goldstein, but he later married his cousin Sylvia, daughter of Yosef's brother Yancze, which warrants further description.

By the early part of the 20th century, Yancze,[17] the third of the five children of Meir and Malka Goldstein, had a prosperous engineering business in Warsaw. Among other innovations, he and his business partner had invented a cigarette-making machine which they exported world-wide. But he and his partner decided to leave Poland following the death in 1920 of his father, Meir, from a stroke brought about by a vicious attack by anti-Semitic hooligans who cut off his beard.[39] Yancze did not want his children to be brought up in such a hate-ridden environment. He was at first planning to emigrate to Canada but travelled first to see family (likely Yosef and Feigele, and Smith) in London. The family persuaded him to stay in London and call for his wife, Choomah,[40] and their surviving children, Abraham (Alf), Annie, Fay, Noah (Nat), and Sylvia; their two other children, Isaac and Yitta, died in Poland at the early ages of one and three respectively. The children were all under 12 years old - Sylvia was the youngest at just seven months. Because they were anticipating emigrating to Canada, their permit specified that country rather than England, so they had to wait in Antwerp to change the permission – it took six months before they could complete their journey. They set up house in Hackney Road, just north of Bethnal Green, with a factory on the ground floor making umbrellas and walking sticks and working for the many Jewish furniture-makers in the area. During WW2, Mick Goldstein would call in to the house in Hackney Road when on leave from the army to see his uncle and aunt, Yancze and Choomah, and his cousins. He and Sylvia found they had much in common, a romantic relationship developed (sanctioned after consultations with medical and religious authorities), and the rest is history…

As the siblings married, so they naturally moved out of Boreham Street. When Esther married Jack Rosenquit they first took a flat in the nearby Victoria Park area. They moved around the country as Jack's career at The British Home Stores progressed – first to Shepherd's Bush, and then to 30 Goldstone Villas, Hove where they rented a maisonette for 30/- (£1.50) a week. Their son, Laurence, was born in Hove. As turned out to be significant, they kept the lease for that property when they moved to Hollinwell Avenue, Nottingham for Jack to take over a store in the city early in 1940. Their second son, Martin, was born there.

Annie married Solly Leboff, one of eight children, and moved to the (then) well-to-do area of Ickberg Road, Clapton. She became very ill, and in due time had to go into residential hospital care. Their daughter, Nita, was then aged 7 and went to stay with the Goldsteins in Boreham Street, while their son, Leon, then aged 2, stayed with an aunt on the Leboff side of the family. Both children went to boarding schools.

Lou married another Esther. Gertie had to end a relationship with a Catholic boy but then found Alf Denenberg, when she took an item for cleaning into the cleaner's shop at which he worked; after a two-year courtship they married and took a shop with living accommodation above in Edmonton.

Jack Goldstein married Sarah (Sadie) Goldberg. And that's another central strand of the story to be told.

THE GOLDBERGS[41]

Gedaliah (also spelt Gedalie) Yosef (or Yusef) Goldberg, was born in Końskowola, in the Lubin Province of Poland, 74 miles southeast of Warsaw, at that time and up until the end of WW1 part of the Russian Empire.[42] Gedaliah claimed to have been born in 1878, as written by his own hand,[41] but the ages of 19th century Jewish immigrants are rarely certain; celebration of birthdays was uncommon, and Birth Certificates did not exist, so no-one could prove (or even know) how old they were or how old anybody else was. Gedaliah's Death Certificate gives his age as 73 years on 22 August 1950, which is inconsistent with a birth date in 1878; he would have to have been born on or before 22 August 1877. Further, his Marriage Certificate (to Leah Kaufman) gives his age as 26 on 16 January 1911, making his birth year as 1885.

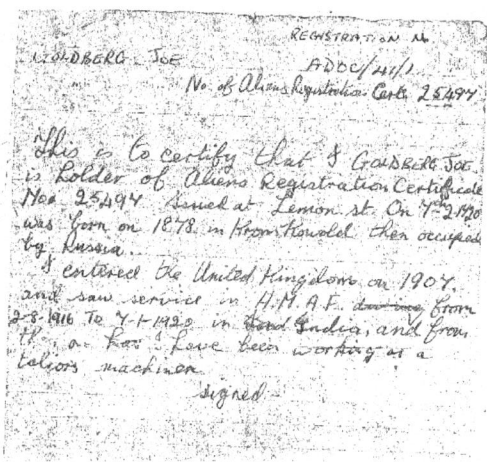

13 - Personal information statement of Gedaliah (Joe) Goldberg

Gedaliah began to use the name of Joe (from his second name of Yosef, or Joseph) when he came to England in 1907 (again, based on his own statement[41]). He made his living as a journeyman tailor (ie employed by someone else), and at the time of his marriage was living at 18 Burdett Road, Mile End.

Joe married Leah Kaufman at the East London United Synagogue on 16 January 1911. Her age is given on the Marriage Certificate as 26 years, suggesting a birth date of 1885. However, when she passed away on 7 September 1929 the Death Certificate gave her age as 41, corresponding to a birth year of 1888.

There are further ambiguities regarding Leah's maiden name. As mentioned, she presented as Leah Kaufman on marriage, but the Birth Certificates of Freda and all four sons Barnet (known as Ben), Ralph, Abraham (known as Sid) and Morris (later known as Ray) all give their mother's name as 'Leah Goldberg, formerly Silver', while her daughter Sadie's Birth Certificate gives Leah's former name as 'Silverman.' It seems unlikely that Leah Silver/Silverman married a man with surname Kaufman before marrying Joe, because her status on the Marriage Certificate to Joe is given as 'Spinster.' Indeed, I have not been able to find a record of such a prior marriage. It therefore remains a mystery as to Leah's differing maiden names on her Marriage Certificate (Kaufman) and on the Birth Certificates of all her children (Silver/Silverman). The name Kaufman would seem to be authenticated by the name given on her Marriage Certificate of her father, Isaac Kaufman (deceased).[43] It has not proved to be possible to locate her Birth Certificate, so it is likely that she was not born in the UK.[44]

By all accounts, the married life of Leah and Joe Goldberg was a struggle against hardship. They were subject to the same seasonal employment problems as were the Goldsteins and all others in the garment manufacturing trade, but as they worked for others, and with little in the way of employment rights, they were regularly out of work with nothing on which to fall back. Despite their evident hardship, their family increased to six children:

- Sarah (**Sadie**)
  Born 17 Sep 1913. Died 7 Jan 2001.
  Married on 25 Jan 1934 Jacob (**Jack**) Goldstein (born 7 April 1912, died 16 Mar 1945); children Leila (1934) and Michael (1939).
  Married on 31 Jan 1948 Aaron (**Alf**) Hyman, born 12 March 1910, died 10 May 1982; child David (1949).

- Barnet (Benjamin, **Ben**)
  Born 20 December 1915. Died 19 Sep 1989.
  Married on 18 December 1937 Ellen (**Nelly**) Florence Fitch (born 20 October 1914, died 7 January 1983); children Leon (1940), Peter (1945), and Trevor (1949).

- **Ralph**
  Born 10 March 1921. Died 16 June 2011.
  Married on 27 December 1940 Leah (**Lily**) Singler (Born 7 February 1921, died 23 May 1952); children Frances (1941) and Judith (1951).
  Married on 3 August 1957 **Joan** Stonebridge (born 19 November 1936); children Kim (1957) and Jeffrey (1962).

- Abraham Shea (Sidney, **Sid**)
  Born 29 June 1922. Died 6 May 1993.
  Did not marry.

- Morris (**Morry**, called himself Mo), changed by Deed Poll to Raymond (**Ray**) Morris Gilbert.
  Born 25 February 1924. Died 24 March 2006.
  Married on 10 July 1949 Kitty Rosenthal (born 6 May 1925, died 18 January 2005); child Stephen (1950).

- Frimet Hanye (or Hantje) (**Freda**)
  Born 21 August 1926. Died 22 Oct 1944.
  Did not marry.

On 2 August 1916, Joe joined the army. He was first a Private (service number 5417) in 3/10th Battalion London Regiment (also known as the London Gurkhas). The 3/10th was the 'third line' of the 10th Battalion and was formed in April 1915; it was based in the UK to provide trained reinforcements to the active 1/10th and 2/10th Battalions. Joe later transferred to 'C' Company of the 1/25th Battalion London Regiment with service number 742022. He

14 - Sadie and Ben as children with their mother Leah and grandmother

15 - Four Goldberg children. From left to right: Ralph (8), Sid (6), Morry (4), and Freda (2)

served as a Cyclist Private in India (arriving 5 March 1917) and the North-West Frontier, where he sustained an injury. The 1/25th Battalion participated in the Waziristan Campaign of 1917; in 1919 they helped quell the Amritsar uprising, and participated in the 3rd Afghan War.[45] Joe returned to the UK and was demobbed on 7 January 1920. He was awarded the WW1 Victory Medal and the British War Medal for service at 'The Frontier Regions of India' between 15 June and 16 August 1917. His collection of medals, however,[46] also includes the 1914 or 1914-15 Star; this suggests he also served in forces against Germany in 1915 or earlier, which would seem to be contrary to his own statement that he joined the army in 1916.[47]

SHALOM, JACK

16 - Joe Goldberg in khaki drill uniform worn by soldiers in the tropics in WW1

17 - London Rifles 'C' Company March 1918. Joe Goldberg is in the third row from the bottom, 5th from the left

17 - Joe Goldberg's army souvenirs: message pouch, medals, sew-on Regiment badge, and badge (or epaulette) for his Small Box Respirator (gas mask)

18 - Joe Goldberg, taken on a march in Hyde Park, London. The reverse says: 'To my loving children J S and L Goldstein' (Jack, Sadie and Leila) but not mentioning me, so must be dated after Leila's birth year but before mine, ie between 1934 and 1939

Leah and Joe Goldberg moved home several times:

- At the time of their marriage (1911) they were both living at 18 Burdett Road.
- Sadie's Birth Certificate (1913) gives an address of 32 Jubilee Street, Mile End.

SHALOM, JACK

- Ben's Birth Certificate (1915) gives an address of 45 Paragon Road, Hackney.
- At the time of serving in the Army, Joe's address was given as 4 Jamaica Street, Stepney.
- Ralph's (1921), Sid's (1922), and Ray's (1924) Birth Certificates have 30 Darling Row Buildings, Bethnal Green.
- The Marriage Certificate of Sadie and Jack (1934) give the address of 30 Cambridge Buildings, Bethnal Green. This is in all certainty the same address as 30 Darling Row Buildings, as Darling Row is a small road off Cambridge Heath Road; the letter from the Metropolitan Asylums Board, Grove Park Hospital to Joe Goldberg, informing him of Leah's death in hospital on 7 September 1929, gives his address as 30 Darling Row, while Leah's actual Death Certificate gives her address as 30 Cambridge Buildings. Moreover, Freda's Birth Certificate gives Joe's address as 30 Cambridge Buildings Darling Row. It is therefore certain that they were one and the same address.
- Ben's Marriage Certificate to Nelly (1937) gives his address as 196 Lower Clapton Road, Hackney, but that is probably not the family home as Ben was a journeyman butcher and certainly after the war was working in Clapton, Hackney.
- Ralph's address on his Marriage Certificate to Lily (1940) is given as 54 Varden Street, Stepney, but this was not the family home as the same address is given for Lily.
- Ray's Marriage Certificate to Kitty (1949) gives his address as 22 Cambridge Heath Road.
- By the time of Joe's death, he was living at 1a Shepherdess Walk, Shoreditch.

Tragedy was to strike the Goldberg family when Leah contracted tuberculosis of the lungs and the kidneys, no doubt due to the crowded and unhealthy conditions in which the family lived. When she passed away on 7 September 1929 aged (according to her Death Certificate) just 41, her eldest child, Sadie was ten days short of her 16th birthday. Joe himself was not in good health and had to work as many hours as he could find employment, so Sadie had to take the major responsibility for bringing up her five siblings – Ben, 13; Ralph, 8; Sid, 7; Morry, 5; and Freda, just a week beyond her third birthday – as well as running the household. She naturally became the 'mother' of the family, and that relationship and bond remained embedded in the family to their last days. It was Sadie to whom the growing siblings turned in times of need, even in adulthood; it was Sadie who continued to look out for her family when problems arose, doing what she could to help them find solutions; it was to Sadie's house that the brothers came when on leave from war service.

Sadie met Jack Goldstein at a social club in 1930 or 1931, when they we still teenagers. She described[10] the meeting as "love at first sight…he cut quite a striking figure, wearing what was then known as 'plus fours'… We started dating and as time went on our love blossomed."

It was some surprise to Sadie to find that her father, Joe, already knew the Goldsteins of Boreham Street, because he was friendly with the Waterman family who lived next door at number 23. It was no wonder that Joe was not keen on a serious relationship developing between Sadie and Jack. Sadie was the backbone of the Goldberg household since her mother died and was bringing up her five siblings. She had looked after Joe during his regular illnesses and kept and managed the family house; to lose her would be a challenge all round. The other children were still dependent on her during her time of courting Jack – Ben was 16 and had left school, but the others were all under ten years old, with the youngest, Freda, just five. However, Joe soon realised that Sadie and Jack were very much in love, and that was all that mattered. Because of the dependency of the Goldberg family on Sadie, her engagement to Jack was longer than they might have wanted, but they married in early 1934 in Bethnal Green Great Synagogue on a grey Thursday afternoon. They enjoyed a modest set tea in Lyons Tea Shop in Bishopsgate, and then the two of them went to a cinema (or 'the pictures' as it was then called) in London's West End. They set up home in rented rooms in Hackney, quite a way from Joe, who now had to bring up by himself four children aged 12, 11, 10, and eight – quite a challenge for him.

Sadie and Jack moved around in their early married years, not least of the reasons being that they fell behind in their rent!

SHALOM, JACK

- When they married in 1934 they rented at 107 Amhurst Road, Hackney, which is also the address when Leila was born that year.

- Sadie recalled to me that at one time we lived in Jenner Road, Hackney.

- When I was born in 1939 we lived at 55 Grantley Street, Stepney.

- By my very early childhood (by about 1941) we were at 60 Fairholt Road, Stamford Hill, Stoke Newington.

19 - Sadie, Jack, sister Leila and me, probably 1943, before Jack enlisted

My first recollections in life are living at 60 Fairholt Road. It was an imposing three-storey semi-detached house, where we rented a few rooms. I can remember the two bedrooms on the top, with Leila and me sleeping in one bed in the inner room, and Sadie in the front room using a rexine-covered 'Put-U-Up.' I say just "Sadie" because from my earliest memories Jack was away at war, in the Royal Air Force Volunteer Reserve (much more of which later). As well as the two bedrooms, we shared a bathroom with the landlords. Two pennies in the slot (2d, worth about 0.8d) gave enough gas through an old geyser to warm half a bath-full of water, which had to be shared! We also had a tiny living room and a scullery off, looking out onto the garden. There was a coal fire in the living room in front of which we took turns for a weekly bath in a 'tin' (zinc-plated metal) bath filled with hot water from a kettle. In winter we wore liberty bodices and wrapped up well against the cold, as there was no other form of heating. On cold nights we wore vests, thick fleecy pyjamas, and bed-socks.

Our landlords, who I think were called Bellchamber (a name I thought very funny at the time), lived on the ground floor and were pretty awful to us. They had a cat and kept chickens, and there was what seemed to me to be a huge cherry tree in the garden, reaching right near to the scullery window. We were not allowed in the garden, and we had to creep around the house so as not to annoy them. They objected to Leila and me having keys to the house – so we had to wait outside the house, in all weathers, when we got home from school, for Sadie to get back from work to get in. For a while we had a key attached to a piece of string hung inside the letterbox, so we could pull it out to gain entry at will, but they soon stopped that. Sadie had to work, of course, when she lost Jack, and probably through the war in any case. She worked in the workshop of Jack's father, Yosef, in the East End. She was a whizz with the needle and had been a dressmaker since leaving school. I remember the Bellchambers complaining that I was at home unattended during the day during the school holidays – what they expected I don't know! I recall one summer holiday, when I was alone in our flat; I had decided to make myself a pin-ball bagatelle – I don't know if such things could then be bought, but we did not have any money for many toys in any case. I got a wooden apple box from the local green-grocer and bought a few pence-worth of nails in Woolworths. We had a small hammer (about the only tool I can recall), and I set to in the scullery, as quiet as I could possibly be. It was not long before I was in trouble, and they gave Sadie a lot of verbal abuse when she came home.

SHALOM, JACK

20 - With Leila outside 60 Fairholt Road, about 1946

There was a cellar, which frightened me but in which we sheltered during air-raids. I can still hear in my head the sirens warning of an expected attack. The cellar was where Mr Bellchamber had a small workshop, and I particularly remember the glue-pot which smelt awful when heated to make it workable. It was also the coal store – coal being delivered from a horse-pulled lorry in large hundredweight sacks (about 50.8kg) and deposited down a manhole just outside the front door into the cellar. The process made everywhere black with coal dust, adding to the terror it struck in me about the place.

All four Goldberg boys served in WW2, and thankfully all returned. As I mentioned, they turned up at our house when they had leave from the army in the war, especially the unmarried ones, Morry (as he then was) and Sid. I remember the excitement when they both managed to get leave at the same time. Morry always amused me, sitting on a kitchen chair in reverse with the chair back between his legs, being really funny and reading my comics! He was full of typical East-End life and Jewish humour – always doing something funny to amuse me, like saying silly things or waggling his ears – he could fold his ear into the ear-hole and release it at will without touching it! After the war, one of them, I think it was Morry, brought home a suitcase of memorabilia – German medals and the like, and for a while I was the envy of my friends; I still have a German field compass amongst my treasures.

Ben married Nelly (Ellen Fitch) before the war (1937) and moved to 5 Oster Terrace, Walthamstow, where they lived for the rest of their lives. It would have been a very difficult time for them, as Nelly was a Christian and, in those days, to 'marry out' of the Jewish religion was almost a sin. Even to date someone who was not Jewish was so frowned upon that many a love affair was crushed by demanding parents. In later generations, inter-marriage became more acceptable in many families. My sister was the first of the Goldstein grandchildren to marry a non-Jew, and she went through a terrible time as a consequence. Sadie soon accepted the situation as she could see Leila's determination and the happiness it was bringing to her, but Leila had to tell her grandparents, who were far less understanding. I recall the day she went to see them in Manor Road to break the news. She was very sternly lectured and given an angry dressing-down which would have deterred many young people. 'Marrying out' led to being disowned by the family in most cases, and that was effectively Leila's fate as far as the Goldsteins were concerned. It is difficult for those not part of such situations to understand the emotions involved, especially from today's perspectives, but those who have seen the movie 'The Jazz Singer' will recognise the anger and grief in Sir Laurence Olivier's dramatic performance when he found his son, played by Neil Diamond, was living with a non-Jewish woman.[48] My own 'marrying out' was less dramatic than Leila's, probably because it was a few years later when integration by marriage was becoming more common. I did not have to break the news to my grandfather, Yosef, as he had passed away by then; Feigele was not pleased but was lovingly understanding, even sending a China tea-set as a wedding gift. Nonetheless I was given a harsh lecture by Esther and received no communications from any others of the Goldstein family – none of them accepted invitations to come to the wedding. Since then, a few others from my and later generations of the Goldstein clan have 'married out,' with far less disapproval then Leila and I endured.

Opposite Ben and Nelly in Oster Terrace lived the large Skevington family, Maggie and Harry with their 11 children - curiously, the same number as Yosef and Feigele Goldstein. I met the youngest daughter, Janet, at the wedding of Leon, Ben and Nelly's oldest son, and in due time she became my first wife.

Ralph married Lily (Leah) Singler in 1940, when they were both 19-years-old. He was a gentlemen's hairdresser at the time (not having yet been called up for the army), a career he maintained for the rest of his working life. They had two daughters, Frances and Judith, and were re-housed after the war to a prefab[49] in Mimosa Road. Shortly after Judith's birth in 1951, Lily was diagnosed with a cancerous teratoma of the ovaries, and developed widespread secondaries in the abdomen; sadly, she passed away in May 1952, aged just 31 years. Frances and Judith were thus brought up by members of Lily's family. Five years were to pass before Ralph married again, to Joan Stonebridge; they had two children, Kim and Jeffrey.

Ray (as he had by then become) married Kitty Rosenthal after the war in 1949 and they settled in Stratford, London. A year later, their son Stephen was born. Ray built a career in the retail garment trade.

Sid was never the same after the war. He could not settle, drifted, and had spells of serious depression and other mental ill health. For long periods he cut himself off from the family – years could go by without his siblings even knowing where he was. I know Sadie was always worrying about him – the little boy she had brought up from the age of seven when her mother had died. And then there would be a call to one of his brothers or Sadie for help, normally for money. His was a human tragedy, born of traumatic experiences in the war, not really understood or recognised in those days, let alone properly helped.

Tragedy was to strike the Goldberg family again, when Freda died in 1944 at the age of just 18 from Addison's Disease, caused by renal tuberculosis. She was unmarried and living in Kensington, London, ironically at 19 Addison Gardens. Not long afterwards, Joe suffered a serious stroke which kept him hospitalised for some time, and thereafter in poor health until he passed away on 22 August 1950.

21 - Goldberg siblings from left to right: Sid, Freda, and Morry

23 - Brothers Ben (left) and Morry (right)

24 - Ralph

25 - Sid

SHALOM, JACK

THE GOLDSTEINS' WAR YEARS[50]

As war became imminent, London prepared. Sandbags were piling up outside civic buildings; Fire Wardens were appointed, Yosef Goldstein being one, and given helmets; gas-masks were issued to school children – made of rubber with a snout where the filter was and with a celluloid visor – all in a cardboard box on a string for the shoulder; rationing was introduced; black-outs were prepared; air-raid precautions distributed. Many people from London, fearing bombing by the Luftwaffe, began to leave for safer places if they could. Jean, then aged 11, was sent to Cardiff with some neighbours rather than being evacuated with the school, travelling in a packed train full of people fleeing the capital.

26 - Yosef Goldstein as a fire guard in WW2

All the boys of both the Goldstein and Goldberg families would soon be fighting for their country. No, it was for much more than that. Their deep-rooted beliefs, their culture and values were under attack like nothing ever before. Although the tragedy and horrors of WW2 were yet to unfold, they knew what was happening in Nazi Germany; anti-Semitism was not unknown, even to those born in England.

As the boys waited for their conscription, and the fear of German bombings gripped the people of London, Feigele and Yosef took Debbie and Ron to stay in Esther's maisonette in Hove (Esther and Jack Rosenquit then living in Nottingham). They used the only transport Yosef could get – an open fish-lorry! At literally the last minute, Debbie's friend Rene Schwartz plus her mother and two

SHALOM, JACK

sisters joined them, all piling in the lorry for the 60-mile journey! Jean was reunited with the family in Hove, returning from Cardiff. Gertie evacuated there too, but after just ten days could not bear the separation from her Alf, so returned to London. Jack's wife Sadie, by then with her two children Leila and me, stayed there for a short while, Jack remaining in London.

After about six months in Hove, the London bombings eased for a while, and Yosef decided the family should return to London. Yosef, Mossy and Mick had remained in Boreham Street, trying to keep the family workshop going while the boys were awaiting call-up. Debbie was allowed to return there too, so as to be near to Alec who had a few weeks before having to report for service duty.

Some weeks after Esther and her husband Jack moved to Nottingham, her husband Jack volunteered and was called up for training with the Royal Army Ordnance Corps.

With her brothers all going into the forces, Polly decided to volunteer for the Women's Land Army. She was initially turned down due to being too small, but a short while later the authorities relaxed the physical requirements and she was accepted.

But by January 1940, the severe bombing of London resumed incessantly every night, especially in the docks area and the City, Bethnal Green included. It was time to leave Boreham Street, made easier by Yosef having already established a larger workshop in a building owned by his brother-in-law, Jacob Smith at the corner of Great Eastern Street, just a few minutes west of Boreham Street.

Yosef and Feigele found a small apartment in Sandringham Road, Dalston, and were soon joined by the family members who returned to London having evacuated to Hove. But as the German air raids became relentless and bombs began to fall over London, the Goldsteins, like thousands of other families, decided they had to leave London altogether. They evacuated first to Dunstable in Bedfordshire, and shortly thereafter to a nearby village, Houghton Regis. For about a year, Yosef and Ron commuted every day to the new workshop. The journey, by war-time public transport was horrendous – bus, two trains, underground, trolley bus – taking two hours each way.

27 - Yosef Goldstein's workshop in Great Eastern Street. Yosef is back centre wearing an apron, in front of a model; to his left in spectacles is Mr Tan, his partner; Jack is on the left at a bench, wearing a tie; Lou is on the right between two women, towards the back at a machine, with Ronnie opposite

Jean and Debbie went to stay with Esther in Nottingham, as did a few other members of the wider Goldstein family and of her husband Jack's family; various relatives and their friends on short periods of leave from the forces also descended on the Nottingham address, so the house was jam-packed. On one Passover, when Jack Rosenquit was on leave, he and Debbie's fiancé Alec, also on leave, had to sleep in the family car!

Gertie and Alf had their first child, Margaret, in January 1941. They decided that London was not the place for a baby, with all the dangers of bombing and the disruption there, so they evacuated to Romford, Essex, renting a house for 25/- (£1.25) a week. Some years later they moved further east to Westcliffe, and later to Thorpe Bay.

Polly's son Paul began his life in a home for evacuee children in Hertford, where Polly had obtained work as a helper. He then lived with a family in Hoddeston when Polly had to go back to London to

SHALOM, JACK

find work at the end of the war. Some years later, when Polly married Wolfie, they went to live in the Goldstein family home at 105 Manor Road, where Polly was already living.

Sadie described being "evacuated to distant parts and seemed to be pushed from pillar to post." There is no record of the details, but I do recall Sadie saying that we all evacuated to somewhere on the King's Sandringham Estate; she was bitter that we were shortly told to leave as Jack was 'a foreign alien,' having been born in Poland, and was presumably considered to be a security risk. Indeed, some years after the war had ended, and it had long been confirmed that Jack had been killed in action, Sadie was as bitter as ever. She had a letter published in *The Mail on Sunday* (22 September 1991), headed 'Hero's reward':

> "My Polish-born late husband, who was shot down over Germany on a bombing mission in 1945, had lived in England since he was four and enlisted in the RAF when the Government decided to recruit 'friendly aliens.'
>
> My children and I were evacuated to the Sandringham estate of Lord and Lady Fermoy. Then one day a local government official called with an order for us to be transferred elsewhere.
>
> Sandringham was a 'restriction area,' he said, and as I had married an alien we should not have been sent there. This indicates just how long disgraceful treatment of Poles has existed."

How ironic that this 'foreign alien' laid down his life for his adopted country a few years later…

While Mossy was serving in the war, he learned that their house had been destroyed in an air-raid. His wife Nita, and their (then) one child, Roy, were unhurt, but this was the signal for them to leave London. They moved to York, near to where Mossy was serving as a PE Instructor, so became re-united. Later, they were joined by some of Nita's family. Roy recalls[18] living with Nita at her parents' home and being bombed out more than once.

28 - Mossy **29 - Debby** **30 - Polly**

Esther decided to return to London to be near her parents and sisters, the brothers all being away on active service. Debbie came up to Nottingham to look after her two boys, Laurence and Martin, while she spent two days house-hunting by taxi in North London. She settled for a large three-storey bomb-damaged house at 105 Manor Road, Stoke Newington, a house that over the following decades was to feature in the lives of all the Goldstein siblings for one reason or another. The agent promised faithfully that by the time she returned with their furniture, the shattered windows would be replaced, the rubble cleared, and water, gas and electricity would be laid on. But it was not so. Three weeks later she arrived with the furniture van to find nothing had been done. It was her brother Jackie[37] who came to the rescue. He and Sadie lived with their two children, Leila and me, just a few minutes' walk away at 60 Fairholt Road. For the next few days, Sadie looked after Esther's two boys, Laurence aged two-and-a-half and Martin aged just one, while her husband Jack helped Esther to do what they could to make the house habitable.

Debbie, who married Alec Lubdofsky (later, Davis) in 1941, stayed at Manor Road when she became pregnant, working as a machinist for as long as she could, before the London Hospital arranged for her to be evacuated to the tiny village of Whitwell, near Hitchen in Hertfordshire for the birth of Barry in August 1942. She was eager to get back to London after that, so went back to live in the top floor flat at Esther's House in Manor Road, where Feigele, Yosef and Jean were then also living. She found a job as a machinist for a dress and suit manufacturer in nearby Fairholt Road, the street in which Jack, Sadie, Leila and I were living, Jack awaiting his call-up into the RAF. Barry spent the day at a small nursery opposite Esther's house in Manor Road; some years later, when Jack was away from home serving in the RAF, and Sadie had to work to make ends meet, I too was a child at that same day nursery before being old enough to go to school.

31 - Mick

32 - Ronnie

33 - Lou

Throughout the time that the boys were serving in the war, their periods of leave, however short, were eagerly awaited by all concerned, and held to be precious times. Sometimes one of the boys managed to get home 'unofficially' and without their families knowing they were coming.

I remember one occasion when Jack came home to us for a birthday - I don't remember if it was mine or Leila's. Our birthdates are only six days apart, so I can pin the date down to around the end of April or the beginning of May. It must have been 1944, because Jack enlisted on 22 January 1944 and was killed in action on 16 March 1945. There was a knock at the door. It was Jack, on leave for the birthday party. I rushed downstairs and raced to the heavy street door. As I struggled to open it, I caught a glimpse of Jack, but only for an instant. In my anxiety to get the door open as quickly as possible it banged against my forehead. An immediate cry, and I

SHALOM, JACK

was in someone's arms (I like to think, Jack's), being comforted. Out came the cold penny and the knob of butter for the bump.... I have no recollection of the party, or indeed of anything else that day. Just a brief glimpse at the person I was never to get to know, never to play with in the park, never to share growing up or being a man. But how that brief glimpse remains in my mind and in my heart.......

34 - Sadie and Jack, probably late 1944 or early 1945. The last family photograph before he was killed

SHALOM, JACK

As the war progressed, raids on London became worse than ever, and the 'Doodle-Bugs' – the frightening V1 and V2 rockets - rained down, Debbie and her small child Barry went to stay to be near her friend Rene Schwartz, who by now had married and moved to the village of Upton, near Greasby, on The Wirral, Cheshire; they were billeted in the nearby village of Upton. A year or so later, Rene decided to move to be near her family who had relocated in Blackpool to get away permanently from the London bombings. Debbie felt isolated, as well as pining for her husband Alec, stationed by this time in Italy. But Rene found a place for her and Barry with a family living near to her in Blackpool, so that's where they stayed until the end of the war.

At around that time, sometime in 1944, Leila and I were evacuated to Blackpool.[51] [52] It was 'Doodle-Bug' time. How dreadfully frightening it must have been for mothers in London, left to look after their children while their husbands were away, somewhere, fighting the war. I recall being just five-years-old, holding Sadie's hand in Stoke Newington High Street, just down from Stoke Newington Railway Station, outside Vale's (private) Library. We had stopped when Sadie met a woman she knew. I heard the friend say something about Stoke Newington School in Church Street. It was where 'they' were arranging evacuation - whatever that meant. Within five minutes we were at the school...

I remember being dressed up in my raincoat with a luggage label bearing my name attached to the lapel, and a 'Mickey Mouse' gas mask round my neck. We were waiting to get on the train, bound for Blackpool - although I don't think I even knew that at the time, and certainly I had no idea at all where it was - and I doubt Sadie knew that much about it either, as she had hardly been out of London all her life. After the train journey we were taken to a large hall – it may have been a gymnasium or community centre – where we had to sleep for the night – rows and rows of children of all ages. In the morning we were put on buses and driven round the streets, stopping now and again for the person in charge to get out and knock on a few doors to see if the occupants would take any of us in. Particularly in today's society, it seems horrific. But that is how it was. As the day went on, all the other kids had got off our bus, leaving just me and my ten-year-old sister Leila with the person in charge. It was getting dark, and the woman must have been getting anxious. As the bus moved on a bit, she got out and knocked on a door. After a brief conversation she was back in the bus and off we went another short distance to another house...and another...and another... It would have been typical of Sadie if the last thing she had said to Leila was not to let me out of her sight; the dutiful daughter stuck to that absolutely. But who would take in two young children, especially of different sexes and five years apart in age? Not many, it was clear. But eventually we found a childless couple who were willing to take on the challenge! And so it was that we entered someone else's world.

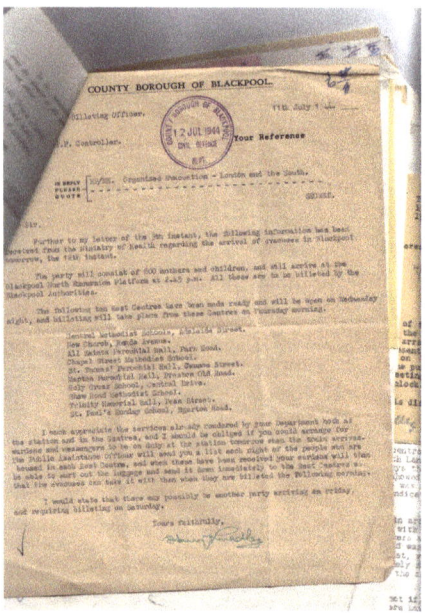

35 - Blackpool County Borough correspondence of July 1944 regarding reception and processing by the town of 800 mothers and children evacuees. Reproduced with kind permission of the Heritage Service, Blackpool Council

It seems impossible now to comprehend that process. A young loving mother, separated from her husband by war, putting her two young children on a train to an unfamiliar town, hundreds of miles away, to be looked after (she prayed!) – and, in reality, brought up by strangers, for ... who knew for how long....? It is incomprehensible by today's standards, where parents don't seem to be able safely to let their kids out of their sights for a minute. But by all subsequent accounts, we were lucky. We were indeed looked after, and even loved. I have a clear memory of lots of tears as we finally left to go back home to London.

It's curious how one remembers little cameos of life so far back in one's memory. I recall the house number was 60 - the same as that of the house in which we lived in Fairholt Road in London. The couple we stayed with were entertainers by profession - one was a singer and the other played the piano, but I can't recall which was which! The mother of one of them lived with them too, and she certainly became my 'Grandma' for the time we were there. I was a bit frightened of their dog, which I think was called Bruce.

The first days at the local school were horrendous. I had only just started school in London but at least there I was with friends. Here in Blackpool I knew no-one, and for the first time in my life I regarded myself as an outsider, not least of the reasons being that I seemed to be the only Jewish person in the class. Boys and girls were segregated even at play-time - I remember my sister and I standing either side of a huge wire fence in the separate playgrounds, sobbing our little hearts out!

But evidently, we got by, and soon began to do the things that all children do...like chalking on a wall on the way home, for which Leila got a roasting from our hosts when she was reported by a neighbour. That was the first time I came across the word 'sulk' - an activity at which Leila was particularly good but which was a no-no in our hosts' house!

Then there was the beach, at the end of our very long road, or so it seemed. We sometimes saw flying boats[53] sweeping along the beaches; collected shells - never seen by either of us before; my first experience of hailstones; being stung by a wasp, and the blue paper remedy....

Sadie came up to see us on occasional weekends. It must have been horrendous for her. Travel (by train, of course) was not easy in those days, priority being given to military users, and how she could afford the fare I don't know. And how heart-breaking to have to go back to the London bombings, leaving your children behind, to an empty home, your husband in mortal danger. I know that this experience was repeated thousands of times across the country, but that doesn't in any way lessen its deep impact on me.

I believe we were living in Blackpool for about two months (for reasons I will give in the next section). When it finally came to leaving, Leila and I went to buy Sadie a gift. Where else to go but to Woolworths; but what to buy? For whatever reason I do not know, but we eventually decided we could afford.... a wooden rolling pin! No doubt this caused great amusement, tempered to be sure by a wish not to offend us. <u>We</u> thought it was a good idea, anyway!

Leaving the family that had taken us into their lives was a trauma for us all. We had naturally grown very fond of them, and as well-brought up children we were so very grateful. But of course, we had the joy of going home and being where we belonged, with Sadie. For the family which had nurtured us at such a formative period of our lives, it must have been dreadful. I know that the couple's mother, 'Grandma', who clearly loved me as if I were her true grandson, cried her eyes out when we finally waved goodbye at the door. It was Saturday 16 December 1944, as I will explain later. How I wish we had kept contact with them. They were so kind and generous beyond belief, and yet I know nothing of what came of them and have never been able to repay them in any way at all. I feel very bad about that.

After Houghton Regis, towards the end of 1944, Feigele and Yosef relocated to Luton, where they lived not far from the Smiths. Esther left Manor Road to join them for a while, commuting daily with Yosef to London – he to his factory in Great Eastern Street, and she to her job in Middlesex Street.

As the war in Europe WW2 finally came to an end, Esther returned to 105 Manor Road with her parents, Feigele and Yosef and youngest sister Jean. That large house replaced Boreham Street as the focus of the Goldstein family home. Feigele and Yosef lived there until Yosef passed away suddenly at the age of 75 on 30 August 1958. He had suffered from heart trouble for several years. Gertie recalls[54] how her mother, Feigele told her that Yosef had leaned forward to turn on the television set when he fell back into her arms. "He died in my arms," she said, "with *liebshaft*, with

36 - From left to right: Jacob Szmidek ('Smith') and his second wife, Ruchze (Rene); Herschel and his daughter Esther; Yosef and Feigele; Yancze and his wife Choomah

37 - Feigele and Yosef, before WW2

38 - Feigele and Yosef, mid-1950s

39 - Feigele, shortly after breaking her arm, aged 90

leibshaft!" [great love]. Shortly after Yosef passed away, Feigele moved to sheltered accommodation not far from Manor Road, courtesy of Smith. She was still fiercely independent and resistant to living with any of her children, but at the age of 90, when she fell from her bed and broke her arm, the family clubbed together and persuaded her to move to a high-quality private Jewish nursing home in Leigh-on-Sea, not far from where Gertie and Alf, Margaret and Gerald, and Debbie and Alec all lived. She was thus able to live out her days in dignity and contentment until she passed away on 15 October 1977, aged 93.

During the war and for some years afterwards, 105 Manor Road was a kind of stopping-off place for several of the Goldstein siblings seeking temporary living spaces until they could sort out something more permanent. It was also where all the Goldstein family came for Passover and other Jewish festivals, celebrations and happy times. It had some large rooms for such family gatherings and was also able to be used as separate flatlets. Many of the Goldstein children lived there for periods – Jean, of course, from her teenage years; Debbie, Alec and Barry, as described above; Polly on return from the Women's Land Army; Ron when he was 'demobbed' (demobilised); and Esther, her husband Jack and their two sons Laurence and Martin. Shortly after Jack Rosenquit came home from active service, the family moved to a 'prefab' in Dynevor Road,[49] a mile or so away near Stoke Newington High Street.

Everyone who has written about their early Goldstein lives, whether Jack's siblings[10] or my generation,[18] speaks very warmly about 105 Manor Road. However, several of my cousins recall the "frightening" toilet seat in the small room down a step off the kitchen – comprising a large wooden plank with a hole in it – as Sharon says: "You always felt you were going to fall down the hole."[18]

These stories of the Goldsteins' evacuations, ours included, were such a disruption to family lives; the endurance of stress and fear; the havoc and devastation of communities – they are typical of the experiences of families across London and beyond. Wives, husbands and loved ones separated from each other for years on end; children brought up without their fathers or mothers. Schooling disrupted, friendships made and soon lost, education fractured. For example, when several houses in Manor Road where they were living at the time suffered direct hits from the bombs, killing 20 people, Laurence and Martin were sent to a Jewish boarding school in Usk, Monmouthshire for 19 months, Esther managing to see them just once every few weeks. Nita and Leon went to a boarding school which was evacuated to Wales when the war began, and then to a succession of other boarding schools across the Home Counties. Jean's schooling after Rochelle Street in Mile End covered Brighton, Nottingham, Derby, Luton, Dunstable, and Houghton Regis before returning to London at war's end; how amazing that she became a top head-teacher and an outstanding educational researcher!

Evacuation aside, life in war-time London was horrific for everyone. The terror of bombing raids that killed and destroyed; the fear and disruption to normal living when the air-raid sirens wailed, causing everyone to go scurrying for safety into cellars, shelters, or the London Underground – at all hours of the night especially; the hardship of travel; the fires, the rubble, the damage of nearly every street in the centre and huge numbers elsewhere; the death or injury to friends and family; the homelessness of those bombed out of their homes; the sheer misery of lack of decent food, and rationing, and queues for what little was available; the constant deep anxiety about loved-ones serving in the forces, not knowing where they were, let alone how there were; the waiting for news; and the distress and grief when the telegram boy or the police came calling, telling of a husband, wife, son, daughter, brother or sister missing, captured, maimed or killed. And then the dreaded flying bombs, the 'Doodle-Bugs' – the V1 and V2 rockets, which droned on their powered flights and then cut-out as the fuel was exhausted, with everyone below holding their breath for the rocket to fall and explode, hoping it was not coming down near them or their loved ones.

But in the end, one-by-one, all but one of the boys came home from the war to rebuild their lives with their families. Lou was a Lance-Corporal in the Royal Army Service Corps from 1944 to 1946. Mossy was a Corporal Physical Training Instructor in the King's Royal Rifle Corps and stationed around the UK between 1940 and 1946; after the war, he and Nita with their one daughter at the time, Sharon, were re-housed to Hainault in Essex. Esther's husband Jack, by then attached to the 8th Army, was sent off to Egypt in June 1941 and did not return for over four years. Gertie's husband, Alf, sustained a foot injury in Normandy which became gangrenous, resulting in him being transferred back to England. Mick enlisted in July 1940, initially serving with the Royal Fusiliers all over the UK

SHALOM, JACK

as a Sergeant Instructor, and subsequently becoming a Sergeant Major in the Royal Artillery; he was frustrated as not himself fighting fascism, so volunteered for the Jewish Brigade[55] on its formation and served with them (as 'Sergeant Mike' to his ex-army colleagues) in Italy until his demob in January 1947. Ron was called up in October 1942, serving firstly as a Wireless Operator in Light Ack Ack in the UK, North Africa, Sicily and Italy, and was later re-trained as a Loader/Operator; he finished the war with the 4th Queen's Own Hussars, and was demobbed as a Corporal in March 1947.

The husbands of Esther (Jack), Gertie (Alf) and Debbie (Alec) also all served in the forces and returned safely.

The one who did not return was my father, Jack.

SHALOM, JACK

JACK THE AIRMAN

Sadie recorded[10] that "Jack always said he wanted to fly." She also told me that Jack tried to enlist in the air force several times in the early part of the war, desperate to fight the Nazi fascist aggression to his race and the country of his forefathers. He was turned down as he was Polish by birth, until October 1943 when the British Government decided to bring into service all 'friendly aliens.'[56] His eldest brother Lou was in the same position.

40 - Lou Goldstein's Alien Registration Certificate, showing an updated photograph, his change of name to Grayson, and his army service dates

On 18 January 1944, Jack was considered by the Number 22 Aviation Candidates' Selection Board (22 ACSB) [sometimes known as the Air Crew Selection Board]. He would have undertaken two days of selection tests and examinations in maths, geometry, English grammar and composition, etc, as well as medical tests and tests for colour blindness, tunnel vision, night vision, further medical examinations and physical fitness tests.[57] These results were presented in a F2171 form, which graded each candidate on their general intelligence, general knowledge, mathematics, English and manual dexterity, as well as levels of courage, determination, initiative, responsibility, interests in flying and ability in team and competitive sports.[57] Jack was deemed to be in the Medical Category 'Grade 1' and he was recommended for training as an Air Gunner.

SHALOM, JACK

41 - Jack, shortly after enlisting on 22 January 1944. The white 'flash' insert in his side cap indicates that he was still in training

However, the prejudice against him as an 'alien' was marked on his Service Record Card:

> *"<u>NON BRITISH PARENTAGE</u>*
> *Mother Polish, Father Polish.*
> *<u>Not to be posted without reference to Section Commander</u>"*

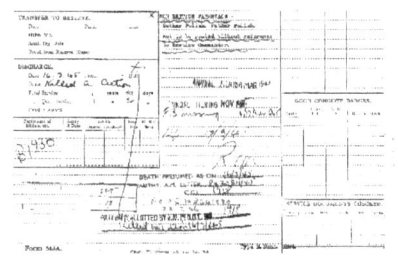

42 - Service Record (side 1), showing personal details including Polish nationality, his slight build, and religion as 'Hebrew'

43 - Service Record (side 2), showing the posting restriction due to being Polish, and the recording of his being killed in action

SHALOM, JACK

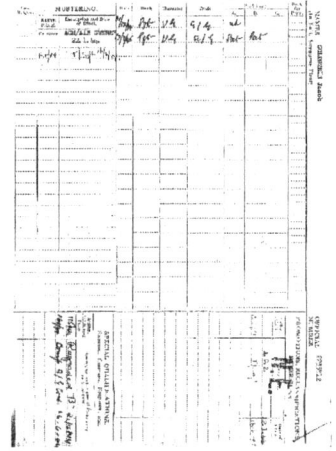
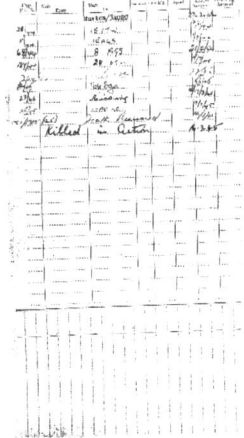

44 - Service Record (side 3), showing Regrading and promotion to Sergeant

45 - Service Record (side 4), detailing postings

Jack's postings were as follows:

- He first reported to the Number 3 Air Crew Recruiting Centre (3ACRC) at Euston on 22 January 1944, the date of his formal enlistment, and was allocated service number 2235812.

- On 12 February 1944 he was sent to the Number 15 Initial Training Wing (ITW).

- He was then trained at the Number 1E Air Gunnery School (AGS) from 1 April 1944.

- Next was the Number 8 Bombing and Air Gunnery School at RAF Evanton, Ross & Cromarty, Scotland[58] from 21 April 1944, when he was regraded 'B'.

- He completed his Air Gunner course on 16 June 1944, being then made (Temporary) Sergeant [T/Sgt].[59]

- On 4 July 1944, he was transferred to the Number 28 Operational Training Unit (OTU) at RAF Wymeswold, Leicestershire.

SHALOM, JACK

- He joined Number 11 Base Unit (1667 Heavy Conversion Unit) at RAF Sandtoft, near Doncaster[60] - on 22 September 1944, when he met up with his crew.

The regular crew of seven comprised:

F/Lt H F (Bud) Churchward	J89440	RCAF[61]	Pilot
Sgt E W (Ted) Hull	3000826	RAF	Flight Engineer
F/Lt J L (Chuck) Goddard	J39384	RCAF	Bomb Aimer
F/Lt L F (Lefty) Etherington	J40412	RCAF	Navigator
Sgt A V (Alf) White	1852534	RAF	Wireless Operator
Sgt J (Jack) Goldstein	2235812	RAF	Mid-Upper Gunner
Sgt R T (Bob) Green	3042364	RAF	Rear Gunner

**46 - The crew of RF154, taken in 1945. From left to right -
Front row: ground crew, Jack Goldstein, Bud Churchward
Back row: Chuck Goddard, ground crew, Alf White, Lefty Etherington, ground crew, Ted Hull, Bob Green**

SHALOM, JACK

I have a very well-worn letter which Jack wrote to his oldest brother, Lou while he was on a few days leave. It is the only item which I have which is in Jack's hand. Like Jack, Lou was born in Poland; as the two oldest boys in the family, they were particularly close.

The letter is dated "Wed 13th". It is possible to pin this down further. During Jack's RAF service, there were only two occasions when 13th of the month fell on a Wednesday - September and December 1944. In his letter, Jack says that on return from leave he was being posted to another station; his service record shows he was posted to 166 Squadron of Bomber Command on 5 January 1945. He also mentioned the possibility of getting more leave around Christmas. I had started at Montefiore House School, Stamford Hill in August/September 1944, and recall spending a significant time in school in Blackpool, so it is unlikely we would be coming home in September. It is therefore pretty certain that the date of Jack's letter was Wednesday 13 December 1944. The text of the letter is as follows (original punctuation etc). I have added some comments in square brackets:

> "Dear Lou
>
> Thanks a lot for your letter which certainly came as a surprise, but was nevertheless welcome. I'm afraid letter writing is not one of my strong points, and if there is one who writes less than you, it's myself.
>
> I am glad to hear you have found yourself a job which must be more in your line than drill and P.T. and that you are feeling quite well. I, myself, am feeling O.K and at present am writing this at home, where I am on leave for a few days. It's a pity your leave does not coincide with mine, but I may possibly get some more leave round about Christmas, and will certainly see you if I possibly can.
>
> I hope your family are in the 'pink'. Leila and Michael will be coming home this Saturday, so don't forget to pop round when you come home and bring the family with you. [This must have been the time when Leila and I returned from evacuation in Blackpool].

SHALOM, JACK

I have been doing a fair amount of flying lately, but nothing very eventful which is how I want it to be. I'm pretty confident I'll get through it all O.K. We've got a very good crew, which is half Canadian and our pilot believes in taking no unnecessary risks. If I had to choose it all over again, I'd still prefer this to the army.

The reason I haven't written my address on this letter is that I am being posted to another station when I come back from leave. I shan't be sorry, as Sandtoft [Lincolnshire], my present station is miles away from anywhere and we hardly leave the camp. We spend most of our spare time playing 1d [one (old) penny] Solo [a card game popular with the Goldstein family], or going to the camp Cinema.

I'm glad to hear you manage to get a bit of time off and visit Brighton dog track, but believe it or not, I've lost all interest in the game and I'm …[words not clear]… certain it will never hold any attraction for me again.

I visited the workshop this afternoon and they have twice as many workpeople, but turn out less than we used to. [The 'workshop' was Yosef's clothing factory in which all the boys worked]. Sadie tells me Dave is rowing [arguing] all day long. [I do not know who 'Dave' is]. They sure miss you on the machine. However, it won't be long now.

Sadie sends her love to you and the family.

All the best,

Jack"

This letter is so poignant. Jack refers to Leila and me coming home (from evacuation); giving up gambling, which was part of the Goldstein family life; the family workshop; and his confidence that he will "get through it all OK," tragically not to be fulfilled.

As foretold in this letter, Jack was indeed posted to another station - Number 166 Squadron of Bomber Command, based at Kirmington, Lincolnshire, on 5 January 1945.[62] [63] [64]

SHALOM, JACK

47 -Flight Crew and ground crew, with Jack in the centre, 1945

Jack's crew was a very close team, and Jack struck up a particularly good friendship with Ted Hull. One evening, Ted and Jack had been out on the town away from their base and arrived at a station fairly late to get back to camp. But there were no more trains that night. They began to walk, but Jack noticed a young nurse also waiting for the train. He spoke to her, and then introduced her to Ted, who rather took to Betty….and eventually they had a happy married life and family.

There are entries in Jack's service record card for 31 December 1944 and 17 February 1945 recording 'V.G.' character and 'Sat.' proficiency in his 'trade' as 'A/G' [Air Gunner].

From 1 February 1945, Jack flew on 16 operations (dates shown in bold) as set out below.[62 64 65 66 67 68]

Date (all 1945)	Jack's Aircraft	Target

1 February	AS-I	Mannheim/Ludwigshafen
Raid by 396 aircraft, including 28 from 166 Squadron, three of which failed to return. Bombs fell in many parts of the town, with 900 houses destroyed or seriously damaged, as well as the railway yards. The fact that only 25 people were killed and 6 injured was likely due to prior evacuation and/or very good provision of shelters. Crew of AS-W and 5 of crew of AS-M were buried in the Commonwealth War Graves Commission (CWGC) Cemetery, Dürnbach (as was, later, Jack).		

| 2 February | AS-I | Weisbaden |

Raid by 495 Lancasters (including 24 from 166 Squadron) and 12 Mosquitos in Bomber Command's one and only large raid on Wiesbaden. There was complete cloud cover but most of the bombing hit the town. There was extensive damage to nearly 1000 buildings, and there were about 1000 people killed and 350 injured. All aircraft from 166 Squadron returned safely.

| 7 February | AS-E | Kleve |

Raid by 285 Lancasters (including 26 from 166 Squadron) and Mosquitos, dropping 1,384 tons of high explosives, to deal with an SS Panzer Armoured Division which was holding up the advance of Allied troops. The mission was successful. After the war, Kleve claimed to be the most completely destroyed German town of its size.

| 8 February | AS-E | Politz-Stettin |

Raid on an important synthetic oil plant by 475 Lancasters (25 from 166 Squadron) and 7 Mosquitos; all from 166 Squadron returned safely, but 12 other Lancasters were lost. Weather conditions were clear, and the bombing was extremely accurate. Severe damage was caused to the plant, which produced no further oil during the war, a big setback to Germany's war effort.

| 13 February | AS-B[69] | Dresden |

Major 500-bomber 'Dresden Raid', part of 'Operation Thunderclap', involving 25 aircraft from 166 Squadron. There were two raids. Group 1, including 166 Squadron, was part of the second raid, three hours after the first; 529 Lancasters dropped more than 1800 tons of bombs with great accuracy. In the first raid, 244 Lancasters had dropped 800 tons of bombs. The effects on Dresden were literally devastating. A firestorm was created and large areas of the city were burned out. The number of casualties is not known with any certainty but might have been 50,000. Jack's crew was flying Lancaster NN770 (coded AS-B for the raid); it released its bombs and was then hit by heavy flak which not only made holes in the fuselage but also blew-back and ignited one of their own incendiaries,[70] causing a considerable fire. This was put out by the Wireless Operator, Alf White, despite him working with very limited oxygen. They then found that the Navigator's log and charts had been sucked out through one of the holes in the fuselage, and instruments were damaged. Even so, Navigator 'Lefty' Etherington brought the aircraft home safely. It did, though, require major repair. Bomber Command losses totalled 6 lost, with 2 more crashed in France and 1 on England. All 166 Squadron aircraft returned to base without any loss.

14 February	AS-H	Chemnitz

Continuation of 'Operation Thunderclap' by 499 Lancasters (24 from 166 Squadron) and 218 Halifax aircraft; 8 Lancasters and 5 Halifax lost. For Jack and his crew, and 15 other crews, the flight began less than 12 hours after returning from the Dresden raid. They were flying AS-H as the crew's normal aircraft, AS-B, was undergoing its major repair. The target area was covered by cloud; many parts of the city hit but most of the bombs fell in open country. One aircraft from 166 Squadron failed to return, nothing being heard from the crew after take-off.

19 February	AS-F	'Fishpond' exercise – test of a radar system
Not counted as an operation.		

20 February	AS-A2	Dortmund

Last Bomber Command large-scale raid on this city by 514 Lancasters (27 from 166 Squadron) and 14 Mosquitos; 14 Lancasters lost including 2 from 166 Squadron (AS-A and AS-D). The southern half of Dortmund was destroyed, as planned.

| **21 February** | AS-E | Duisberg |

Last major Bomber Command raid on Duisburg, involving 362 Lancasters (22 from 166 Squadron) and 11 Mosquitos; 7 Lancasters lost and 3 crashed behind Allied lines in Europe. This was a successful area-bombing raid and much damage was caused. All 166 Squadron aircraft returned safely.

| **23 February** | AS-B (2) | Pforzheim |

First and only heavy area-bombing raid of the war on Pforzheim by 367 Lancasters (23 from 166 Squadron) and 13 Mosquitos plus a Film Unit Lancaster; 10 Lancasters lost, including AS-L2 (5 crew buried at Dürnbach) and 2 more crashed in France. Bombing (1825 tons in 22 minutes) from only 8000ft, was particularly accurate and very severe damage was inflicted. An estimated 83% of the town's built-up area was destroyed, probably the greatest proportion in one raid during the war, with 17,600 people killed – probably the third heaviest air-raid death toll in Germany during the war (after Hamburg and Dresden). 10 Lancasters lost and two more crashed in France. AS-B was in combat with a Junkers JU88 night-fighter over the target.

| 26 February | AS-B | Cross-country exercise |

Not counted as an operation

| 28 February | AS-B | Nuess, Düsseldorf |

AS-B recalled. Not counted as an operation.

| **5 March**[65] | AS-B | Chemnitz |

Continuation of 'Operation Thunderclap' involving 760 Halifax, Mosquito, and Lancaster aircraft (26 from 166 Squadron). The round trip would be for almost 1800 miles, requiring full fuel loads of 2150 gallons. Bomb loads were

8600lb. The operation started badly when 9 aircraft crashed near their bases soon after taking off in severe icy conditions. One Halifax from 426 Squadron crashed in York due to icing, killing some civilians. 22 further aircraft were lost in the main operation - 14 Lancasters and 8 Halifax. Jack's aircraft RF154 AS-B was piloted by Flt Sgt Moore as Flt Sgt Churchward was indisposed; the aircraft returned early before reaching the target due to an unserviceable fault with the rear turret.

7 March	AS-B	Dessau

26 aircraft from 166 Squadron plus 505 others carried out the first raid of this industrial town in the far East of Germany (round trip of 1850 miles). Fuel and bomb loads were the same as for the Chemnitz raid. 18 Lancasters lost, 3.4% of the force. This was a devastating raid on a new target in Eastern Germany with town centre, residential, industrial and railway areas all being hit. AS-B returned with its 2000 lb bomb still hung up in the bomb bay.

8 March	AS-B	Kassel

26 aircraft from 166 Squadron plus 236 other Lancasters and 14 Mosquitoes carried out the last large RAF raid on this target. Unsuccessful due to target being covered by cloud. One Mosquito was lost, but all from 166 Squadron returned safely.

11 March	AS-B	Essen

25 aircraft from 166 Squadron plus 1054 others (largest number sent to a target up to then), dropping 4661 tons of bombs through cloud in daylight. The attack virtually paralysed Essen, with most of the city now in ruins. Some 7000 people had died in air raids. The pre-war population of 648,000 had fallen to 310,000 by the end of April 1945; the rest had left for quieter places in Germany. 3 Lancasters were lost, but all aircraft from 166 Squadron returned safely.

12 March	AS-B	Dortmund
28 aircraft from 166 Squadron in a total of 1108 aircraft – a record for a single target in the entire war. A record 4851 tons were dropped through cloud in daylight. 2 Lancasters were lost, but all aircraft from 166 Squadron returned safely.		

13 March	AS-A2	Erin Benzol plant, Herne and Gelsenkirchen
Raids by 195 Lancasters (18 from 166 Squadron) and 32 Mosquitos. The Gelsenkirchen attack was successful (1 Lancaster lost), but not the Herne raid (all aircraft returned safely).		

14 March	AS-B	Practice bombing trip
Failed to complete due to bad weather. Not counted as an operation.		

15 March	AS-B	Practice bombing trip
Failed to complete due to bad weather. Not counted as an operation.		

16 March	AS-B	Nürnberg
Jack's fateful last flight. Take-off of 26 aircraft from 166 Squadron commenced at 1700 hours, joining 267 others. Nürnberg was a difficult target, being very heavily defended, with at least five night-fighter airfields in the area. It became a long and hazardous trip, as German night-fighters found and infiltrated the main bomber stream even before they reached the target, which was focussing on the railway yards. This was the last heavy Bomber Command raid on Nürnberg, but it proved to be disastrous for 1 Group, which lost 24 of its 231 Lancasters; 3 of these losses were from 166 Squadron as described in the history of 166 Squadron:[66] AS-O, AS-M		

SHALOM, JACK

(particularly harrowingly and dramatically portrayed), and Jack's AS-B, RF154. The story of Jack's loss is given in detail in the next section.

48 - Jack with Bob Green by the rear gun turret

49 - Alf White in the astrodome

50 - Jack in full flying gear

51 – Taken from the astrodome. Jack in his mid-upper gun turret on the way to a daylight operation over Essen, 11 March 1945, just five days before he was killed

SHALOM, JACK

THE LAST FLIGHT OF RF154 ('TARFU')

As already mentioned, there have been several accounts of the final flight of RF154 which resulted in Jack's death.[2-8] All derive, albeit often without due acknowledgement, from the extensive research[7] carried out by my uncle, Ron Goldstein, Jack's youngest brother, and my own posts[8] to the BBC website 'WW2peopleswar' based on this research. I have also published my own version in a joint biography with my Aunt Jean Lawrence (Jack's youngest sister) and cousin Susy Stone (daughter of Jack's brother Mick).[11] But this is the first full and comprehensive account focussing on Jack, incorporating more recent information. It is a fascinating story, demonstrating the phases of war: the courage, the tragedy, the suffering, the personal consequences, the reconciliation….

I base this section on the narrative set out by Ron Goldstein,[7] with his permission, of course. It reconstructs the events in question chronologically. Ron's full research report is an amalgam of various articles, numerous extracts from letters, a multitude of telephone conversations, interviews, dozens of acquired documents, and more. It is set out in ten Chapters, but only the first two are of specific relevance right here, where I focus on the transcript of tape recordings taken by Ron of four surviving members of Jack's crew, Alf White, 'Lefty' Etherington, Ted Hull and 'Bud' Churchward; they are all strictly first-hand reports. I have applied only a light editorial touch but added several explanatory notes. It starts with Alf White's story of events.

> *[ALF]* "March 16th, 1945 was just another day for me and my crew on 166 Squadron based at Kirmington, Lincolnshire. March 14th and 15th had been spent on two short practice bombing trips, which, owing to bad weather, we failed to complete. We were having a late-ish lie-in on 16th March, anticipating perhaps that the bad weather might stop any ops. on that day, but about mid-morning, the inevitable AC/2 came around on his pedal cycle and warned us to be at Briefing immediately after lunch, for our fifteenth[71] and what turned out to be our last operational trip.

SHALOM, JACK

"Ours was a close-knit crew, consisting of

Bud Churchward, the Pilot, RCAF.
Lefty Etherington, the Navigator, RCAF.
Chock[72] Goddard, The Bomb Aimer, RCAF.
Me, Chalky White, the Wireless Operator, RAFVR, from High Wycombe, Bucks.
Ted Hull, Engineer, RAFVR. from Romford.
Jack Goldstein, the Mid-Upper Gunner, RAFVR, from Stamford Hill, and
Bob Green, the Rear Gunner, RAFVR from Barnsley.

52 - From left to right: Ted Hull, Jack, and Bob Green

53 - From left to right: Bud Churchward, Bob Green, Jack, and Ted Hull

"We were billeted in adjoining huts which were dispersed amongst small fir trees, about a mile away from the 'drome'.

"After our call from the AC/2, Bud, Chock and Lefty came into the billet and joined the rest of us, and after once again admiring our selection of pin-ups and running through our crew song 'The Lady of the Manor', we departed for lunch at the Messes, arranging to meet afterwards to wander down to Briefing.

"We all walked past the 250lb high-explosive bomb that had lain beside the path from the Messes for as long as I could remember, arrived at the Briefing Room, and checked that our crew was on the day's 'blood-sheet'. As always, the object of our unwelcome attention for that night remained

SHALOM, JACK

hidden behind the curtains, and there was speculation as to where it might be, but this was soon answered by the arrival of the C.O., Wing Commander Vivian, the Bombing Leader, and the Gunnery Leader. The curtains were pulled aside and there it was revealed, the red tape dog-legged from Kirmington to Reading, the turning point, and on across the Channel, across France to Nürnberg - not a happy sight, as it was well known that Nürnberg, the seat of Nazism, was heavily defended."

54 – 166 Squadron Order of Battle No. 232, 16 March 1945

[LEFTY] "Our target was Nürnberg on the night of 16 March 1945. At briefing we were told to expect moderate to heavy flak with a possibility of fighters before the target.

[ALF] The C.O. and the various leaders gave their usual pep talks and take-off was timed for about 5pm. Off we trooped to the crew room to kit up and snatch a quick cup of tea. Kitted-up, we then joined two or three other crews, in the 'blood wagon' to be taken out to dispersal, where Lancaster B for Baker ('TARFU' to us – 'Things are Really F***** Up') was waiting for us, with Bob, Buster and Stan, our ground crew.

"All the crew were sorry that we had been told to remove the painting of the naked lady on the side of the Lanc., but apparently this offended the WAAFs as we taxied past Flying Control, as a bomb was shown as coming from a very strategic place!

"We made our pre-flight checks and before long the 'green' went from Flying Control and we started up. No sooner were we away when - owing to a change of wind - the runway was changed from the long one to the short one and a lot of mutterings ensued because we were all well aware that we were fully laden with 2154 gallons of petrol and our bomb load. It was going to be difficult to get off the short runway and, allied to this, we knew that the bomb dump was just a few yards to the port side at the end of the runway. The change of runway delayed things, and as we joined the stream of aircraft awaiting the green to go, there were mutterings from Ted, the Engineer, as the Merlins[73] began to overheat. Our turn to go at last came and we taxied on and, as always, I said my very short prayer, "God, please bring us back!". We got the green from the caravan and off we went. At full blast, the four Merlins carried us along the runway and as the perimeter track loomed nearer, I thought, "Christ, we are not going to make it!" But with the last bump as we hit the perimeter track, we got air-borne, and off we went."

[TED] "On the night of the 16th we took off from Kirmington with a 4000 lb Cookie[74] and lots of incendiaries,[75] and experienced trouble with the rear turret when it started to fire spontaneously as we left the runway.[76] The firing mechanism was switched off by the Rear Gunner and the Skipper and I discussed whether I should attempt repairs in flight; but he decided he couldn't spare me from the cockpit or having the rear turret unmanned for what could be a long time. I mention this because it meant that the Rear Gunner's reaction time was extended by having to switch the firing mechanism on again if attacked."

[ALF] "We were all tense on the way out and our crew song was always reserved for coming home, but this time it was not to be.

"We joined the gaggle (no one could describe it as a formation) of aircraft and successfully rounded the turning point over Huntley & Palmer's Biscuit factory at Reading - always a danger spot in my mind - and headed out across the English coast. Being the Wireless Operator, my duties were not too strenuous, and all I had to do was to listen out for the bombing winds[77] and any change of plans. These were usually transmitted in at about 12 words per minute and presented no difficulty to me."

[LEFTY] "Everything was going well until we crossed the French-German border, a few miles south of Strasbourg. Then the rear turret guns kept firing short bursts. The firing solenoid had packed up so the Tail Gunner had put them on to 'Safe'. As we approached Stuttgart on a course of approximately 030°, the Skipper said he was altering course to dog-leg around it, as they were pooping up a lot of flak. We passed Stuttgart without further trouble and got back on track. Then we altered course to approximately 096° for our run in on the target, which was the central marshalling yards. As soon as we had altered course, the Rear Gunner started reporting fighter flares on both port and starboard. Then kites [aircraft] started going down all around us.

"I logged five then quit to take pictures of the H2S[78] screen as we were 14 miles from the target. I adjusted the gain control and set the range dial. The target was showing up perfectly. I looked at my watch noting it was exactly 9.30[79] and as we were due on the target at 9.34 I figured we'd be just about spot on."

[ALF] "Everything went well en route except for a bit of flak and we crossed from France into Germany. That night,

the BBC was broadcasting an account of a fight between Roderick and Danahar,[80] and in my position I was able to tune in and listen, but I was unable to hear the result because the last bombing wind was due at 9.30pm, and by then we were nearing Nürnberg. I obtained the bombing wind and passed it to Lefty and then, as we approached the target, Bud told us to clip on our chutes. On the inter-com. I listened to Bud, Lefty and Chock talking, and I could see the 'Wanganui' flares[81] being put down by the Pathfinders over Nürnberg. We started our run up to the target at 20,000 feet and I could see the flak exploding all around."

[TED] "We were on the approach to the target (Nürnberg) but had not yet opened the bomb doors. The target was in flames and there was some flak ahead but none in our vicinity. A good indication the fighters were about, when the Rear Gunner shouted: 'Corkscrew Skipper for Christ's sake.'"

[LEFTY] "Then it happened -- the Tail Gunner yelled: 'corkscrew starboard.' Just as we started our dive to starboard, I heard the 0.50s in the rear turret open up and then slugs started hitting our starboard wing creeping towards the fuselage and bomb bays containing a 'Cookie'[74] and six 1000lb incendiary clusters. Someone screamed, probably our Mid-Upper Gunner [Jack], and I looked at the floor to see it starting to melt along the side of the fuselage underneath my table. The incendiaries had caught fire.

"I heard Jack say 'Corkscrew p......' He was obviously going to say port but he didn't. All that came out was 'p' and it was several seconds before the Tail Gunner yelled 'Corkscrew starboard'. I believe it was several seconds before Bob Green sounded out. I also feel we were hit with a (Junkers) JU 88 [night-fighter] with upward firing guns. They had them then. They homed in on the H2S[78] transmission. They flew immediately under the bomber stream and the guns fired automatically. Because of Jack's incomplete command, I felt at that time, and still do, that he was hit in the turret and didn't get out. The hydraulics were also damaged. In the rear turret the 0.5 guns elevated and jammed Bob's foot, so he couldn't get out. He manually cranked his turret around to beam, opened the turret doors, leaned out and pulled the ripcord. The 'chute' pulled him out with his boots left in the turret."

[TED] "Apparently it was a JU88, which was already firing at us, and all I could see were the cannon shells ripping into the fuselage on the starboard side below Jack's position and into the wing root which caught fire. My intercom was cut off in the attack, so I had no further contact with the rest of the crew. I shut down the starboard engine, which was in flames, and operated the fire extinguisher for the same, but could not observe the results as by this time there was fire at my position and the floor was melting due to the incendiaries having ignited. I noticed that the front escape hatch had been jettisoned and the Bomb Aimer had gone, indicating that the Skipper had instructed us to bail out.

"My position was up front with the Skipper, so I couldn't see Jack, as the mid-upper turret was over half-way down the fuselage, and he would bail out of the normal entrance towards the tail, as would the Wireless Operator and possibly the Rear Gunner if he couldn't get out over his guns."

[ALF] "We were within a few seconds of 'bombs gone' when, with an almighty crash we were hit in the bomb bay and port wing. From my vantage point in the astrodome[82] I saw that we were on fire, that the port wing was well alight, and some foreign object had come through the bomb bay. It was only too obvious that this was our 'lot', and Bud said: 'Get out quick!'

"My point of exit was the rear entrance door, and it did not take long to climb over the main spar and make my way to the door. I had to pass under Jack's turret, and on my way I slapped his legs[83] in case he hadn't heard Bud's order."

[LEFTY] "I called the Skipper saying: 'Skip, the bomb bays are on fire.' He said: 'Can you put it out?' I replied: 'Hell no!' And with that he said: 'OK boys, bail out.' By this time, the fire had really gained headway and my table was on fire. I swung around to the forward edge of the bench and started putting on my 'chute.' It went on the left clip okay, but the oxygen tube stopped it and one of the elastics caught in the clip. I took off my helmet and unhooked the oxygen tube and after what seemed like hours I freed the elastic and clipped my chute on.

"By this time the flames were coming up on my right side and I knew I was getting scorched, but I couldn't feel any pain. I scrambled past the Skipper who was still at the controls trying to keep it on a steady keel, down into the Bomb Aimer's compartment where the escape hatch was located. By the light of the flames I could see the escape hatch door jammed upright in the hatch.[84] I tried in vain to move it, as the slipstream was holding it fast. Then I decided to drop through the front half of the hatch. I dropped until my chute jammed against the edge. I thought I'd bought it then and there, but I prayed, cussed, swore and pushed and dropped into space. All this happened in approximately one minute from the time we started to dive."

[BUD] "After we were hit and the aircraft was on fire, and Ted and Alf and Chuck had done all they could to put it out, the extinguishers were empty. I gave the emergency jump order. I watched the ones leave who went out the front escape hatch but Jack and the rest were to leave by the rear door, so I couldn't see who left. After I thought they were all gone, I gave a roll-call to check, and I did get an answer from Bob Green only. He was stuck in the rear turret. After he told me he was going I again asked if everyone was gone

before I left. Not hearing any more, I assumed everyone had jumped."

How wrong he was! But in reality, there was little he could have done in any case. If Jack had managed to get out of the burning aircraft, all would have been well and good; if he was already dead (as now seems probable) then there was no point in Chuck doing anything but get out himself; if Jack was so injured that he could not respond, there was very little Chuck could have done to save him.

55 - Aerial view of crash crater, taken by Allies, 9 April 1945

German night-fighter claims records[85] show that at 9.31pm on 16 March 1995, a Lancaster bomber was shot down by Feldwebel (Sergeant) Schuster from Luftwaffe *Nachtjagd* [literally, Night Hunter] unit I./NJG5, based north of Nürnberg. By all accounts, his aircraft was a Junkers JU88G-6. The Lancaster crashed near Kammerstein, which is in the administrative region of Roth, Bavaria, south of Nürnberg. This seems very likely to be RF154, from the timing and the location.

56 - German fighter claims 16-17 March 1945

However, according to 'The Nachtjagd War Diaries Vol. 2' by Dr Theo Boiten, a very respected and thorough researcher for Luftwaffe night fighter claims,[86] the German fighter aircraft which was responsible was probably one flown by Maj Herbert Lütje.

In an effort to determine which of these version is correct, I obtained the views of someone described by Kelvin Youngs as the best authority on such matters, Rod MacKenzie (indeed, it was Rod who provided the map used in Boiten's publication[86]). The essence of Rod MacKenzie's reply is as follows:

> Lancaster RF154 crashed in Luftwaffe grid square TB-9. There were five known claims made in this area, two of which refer to RF154:
>
> - By Maj. Herbert Lütje of 47 Sqn Night Fighter Wing 6. Claim: Lancaster, at 30 km. SSW of Nürnberg: altitude 4,500 m at 21.33 hours. Probably 166 Sqn Lancaster RF154, 12 Sqn Lancaster PD275 or 576 Sqn Lancaster ME317

- By Sergeant Emil Weinmann of 11 Sqn Night Fighter Wing 6. Claim: Lancaster at SW of Nürnberg: altitude 5,000 m at 21.35 hours. Possibly 166 Sqn Lancaster PA234, 625 Sqn Lancaster RF145, or 170 Sqn Lancaster ME307 [there may be some confusion as to Squadron numbers]. Note that this is recorded as a certain victory but is in disagreement with the logbook of the Pilot Weinmann.

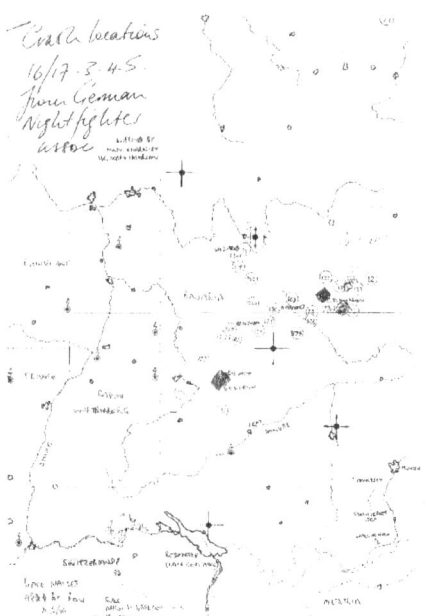

57 - Crash locations 16-17 March 1945

Rod MacKenzie goes on to say:

"I'm afraid that barring the discovery of some contemporary German document that conclusively identifies the claimant of the Lancaster (and I doubt such a document still exists), then there is no way to determine who shot down RF154. I have examined the details of this raid on 16-17 March 1945 in considerable detail and the best that can be done is to narrow down the possible Luftwaffe claimant to perhaps four or five different crews. Most of the German claims were of a very general nature with regards to the location, and there was over-claiming by the Night Fighters on this night.

"I would…be very sceptical if anyone in the future [says] that such-and-such Pilot brought down the Lancaster, as this occurs a lot with some researchers based upon incomplete evidence and unsound reasoning.

"To illustrate the over-claiming by Luftwaffe Pilots, the Boiten publication[86] identifies claims by the Night Fighters amounting to 41 Bomber Command aircraft destroyed, even though only 29 aircraft were lost."

I am, however, persuaded by the fact that RF154 is not listed in a Luftwaffe historical record as one of the aircraft claimed to have been shot down by Maj Herbert Lütje.[87] So while there is always some uncertainty, my inclination is to believe that Jack's Lancaster RF154 was shot down by Feldwebel (Sergeant) Schuster.

SHALOM, JACK

AFTER THE CRASH

All six survivors of Jack's aircraft crew were captured by the German forces. Ron Goldstein's comprehensive report[7] sets out the individual accounts of the four surviving crew members, Alf White, 'Lefty' Etherington, Ted Hull and 'Bud' Churchward, describing their capture by the Germans, being taken to Munich, Nürnberg and the prisoner-of-war camp at Moosburg, before liberation by Americans and their return home. They are harrowing and challenging stories, which warrant reading, but are simply summarised here.

Alf White was captured immediately, as his parachute took him onto the lawn of Nürnberg Prison! 'Lefty' Etherington landed about ten miles south-west of Nürnberg (his reckoning is likely to be reliable as he was the Flight Navigator); he was significantly burned, and by the next morning (17 March 1945) was badly in need of medical attention, so he gave himself up to a small village near to Kammerstein. Ted Hull was also seriously burned about the face and was captured early the next morning (17 March 1945). All three (Alf, 'Lefty' and Ted) were taken to Munich for interrogation and then to Nürnberg prisoner-of-war camp, as were 'Chuck' and Bob.

Bud Churchward was not captured for several days but ended up in a prison in Stuttgart before being marched east. He was liberated by the US Army and did not meet up with the rest of the surviving crew until his return to England.

In this detailed narrative of Ron's[7] is one aspect of Ted Hull's story which was the subject of a letter from Ted to Ron, dated 22 January 1996. Some of the letter repeats the description of the crew and the story of the flight, but there are parts that were startling to Ron in his research and are given in extract here:

> "Dear Ron,
>
> Very pleased to receive your letter asking about your brother Jack….

SHALOM, JACK

…One of the reasons I was pleased to receive your letter Ron, is that for some time I have been in a quandary regarding the events of that night and the following days….

….[After Bud had given the emergency jump order], I moved down in the nose and bailed out, saw our tail wheel pass over me (I was on my back) then I must have hit something, for I came to suspended from my parachute which I have no recollection of releasing from its pack and suffering from burns to my face, broken teeth and pain in my back and side, then lost consciousness again and woke up in a ploughed field adjacent to a forest into which I crawled to wait for dawn. When it was light enough, I used my escape map and compass and set off through the trees but it was not long before I heard voices and concealed myself in some bracken. They passed me by, all but one, and he was aiming a rifle at me, so there was nothing to do but stand up with my hands on my head.

They eventually left me with an old chap with a luger pistol who marched me off across field after field and eventually through a hedge into a hutted camp at the side of a forest and on rising ground.

To my right between myself and the forest was a large pit (100' x 40'?) newly dug and being worked on by people in prison garb. Further along on the same side was what looked like a refilled pit of the same size, then further along still and higher up the rise was another pit with people in uniform moving around it and there was the sound of small arms fire. There were Gestapo and SS men around as well as some in the drab army uniform.

I was then taken into one of the large huts and noticed some of the army men showing each other items of jewellery etc to each other as they came through the door. I built a picture in my mind and became very frightened. Was then taken into a room where two SS officers were seated at a round table and they indicated I should take a vacant place. They questioned me in the expected manner at first but said 'You are a Jew to come from a Jewish Squadron.' This I denied

SHALOM, JACK

but they persisted and said, 'Your Mid-Upper Gunner is a Jew and so are you.' This kept on for about an hour and then I was locked in a log cabin like a cell about the size of a garden shed with bars on the windows. As you can imagine, by this time I was in a state of shock and I've no exact idea how many days I was in that camp. Three times they interrogated me along the same lines and on one occasion while I was in the cell I heard various voices and on looking out of the bars observed a small group of people with armed guards moving towards the pits. My view was from the side but to this day I'm certain one of them was Jack. He was very distinctive as you well know and not easy to miss.

I'm very sorry Ron if this is the first you've heard of this but I think that 50 years ago it was right not to further your Sister in law's grief. I've told several people in recent years including Mr Mark Charnley, who is virtually our Squadron historian, who asked me to let him have a copy of what I'd written, but as it seemed impossible to find his widow this is the first written words I've passed to anybody.

I did try to visit Jack's widow in 1945 but what with being in and out of hospital at that time. But that is another story…

Well, thank, you once again for writing to me, you've taken a load off my shoulders as it were. Don't hesitate to write or phone or call in at any time.

Yours faithfully

E. W. Hull

Ted

The implications of Ted's astonishing story, apart from the issue of war crimes and violation of the Geneva Convention,[88] was that Jack had survived the crash, had been taken prisoner by German forces, and probably murdered at the camp Ted described. Ted was adamant that his account was true.

Later that year, on 1 September 1996, Ron met up with Ted and questioned him about his account. Ted stuck by his story of seeing

92

SHALOM, JACK

Jack at the camp where he was first taken after being captured on 17 March 1945, the morning after the crash. Ron recorded the interview, and the following are extracts from the transcript.

> "[As I arrived at the camp]....a Gestapo gentleman came towards me as we came through the hedge...And then he threatened me 'cos my hands were on my head and I'd lost all feeling and one fell away, and he took a back-handed swipe at me. He didn't really connect, but just bowled me over a bit.... he saw what I was – you know what I mean as we were hated, and then they took me from there into one of these huts on the left for interrogation. I was standing in the corridor at one time outside the door of one of the rooms in this hut and I could see people from the other end coming in - German soldiers, showing each other items that they'd obviously just come by. Then, anyway, I was then taken into this hut and interrogated, and it started off with the normal interrogation you would expect, and I gave name, rank and number and whatnot, and they carried on and they said: 'You're a Jew.' I obviously said I wasn't because of what they did. I could have been mistaken for a Jew because I was swarthy and dark brown hair and tanned up all the time. And next they came at me: 'Your Mid-Upper Gunner is a Jew and so are you.' So, I thought, well, if my Mid-Upper Gunner *is* a Jew I assumed that they'd got him, and also, they must have him because how did they know he was the Mid-Upper Gunner because he would only have an Air Gunner's brevet on [ie he could have been the Tail Gunner]? They were emphatic about that, you see, so we stuck to this. Anyway, I think it was roughly three times they had me in for interrogation, by which I timed with the things that I had seen.

> ".... before they interrogated me, they did plaster my burnt face up with some sort of paste, and wrapped my head in paper bandages, which by this time, what I'd seen [pits being dug by prisoners and the sound of gun fire] and the cross-questioning about making me a Jew, I was getting really frightened. And this went on for a bit, and then I was put in a cell which was like an 8 x 5 garden shed built out of

SHALOM, JACK

logs…. there was a low bench on one side which enabled me to lay down, but that was all there was [in the cell]. [There was] a barred window on the opposite side to the bench. Now this barred window faced out onto the route they brought me in from where the pits were, and I don't know, once again on time, one or two days.

"…. [It was] the very next morning [after the crash that] they were talking about the Mid-Upper Gunner being a Jew.

"So, I heard this noise – commotion – and I looked out, and there were a few people being escorted, if you like…. towards the pits, the pit in question where the firing was going on. I couldn't see from where I was because of where my cell was.

"…. [One of the people being escorted looked like Jack] hadn't got his RAF uniform on, it was the drab sort of garb they'd all got on….I don't think [it could have been somebody else] 'cos knowing Jack, he's very distinctive, although I only saw him virtually from the side he was on this corner of the group, and he was the right height…. he wasn't tall.[89] I am certain I would know Jack even from the rear, and I'm still convinced to this day that that was Jack."

Despite Ted's conviction, his story does not stand up to the evidence in any way at all, as set out below. His account of his capture and interrogation is no doubt accurate; as will be seen later, the German authorities had Jack's body by the time Ted was interrogated. They thus knew he was a half-wing Air Gunner from his breast insignia on his battledress tunic, and that he was Jewish from his identity tags (which stated religion on the reverse). Jack's surname was also a give-away; he had refused to change his name before enlisting, unlike many other Jewish servicemen, no doubt too proud of his heritage.[90] As Ted's ordeal with his German captors went on, the effect of food and sleep deprivation, combined with tough, frightening questioning, repeatedly being challenged, no doubt aggressively, would clearly be putting him under huge stress, and probably delirium. It is very understandable that he might have been confused and even hallucinating at the end of it all, when looking out of his cell window. I myself met Ted (and his wife,

Betty) a couple of times in the late 1990s at his family home in the village of Martin Hussingtree in Worcestershire and found him to be a wonderfully sensitive and gentle person, totally honest and of the highest integrity. He was still bewildered by the conflict between his apparent memories and the irrefutable factual evidence Ron had collated.[91]

The evidence is absolute that Jack did not bail out but crashed still inside the burning aircraft. Through his persistent enquiries, Ron Goldstein received letters from the Ministry of Defence Air Historical Branch 5(RAF) dated 4 June 1996 and 27 March 1997, from which the following are taken, given chronologically:

> "An Investigation Report, dated 6 December 1946, from the No. 3 Missing Research and Enquiry Unit, British Armed Forces of Occupation, to the Air Ministry London, relating to Lancaster Mark I, Serial No. RF154, contains the following information:
> 'Herr Koelisch, [from] Pfaffenhofen, near Roth [about 7 miles SSE of Schwabach] was detailed on 17 March 1945 [the day after the night Jack's aircraft was shot down] by an Officer from the Luftwaffe Station at Roth to proceed to the New Cemetery at Schwabach and bury seven English [sic] Flyers — the dead members of two crews who crashed near Schwabach in the evening of 16 March 1945. Six of these flyers were brought to the churchyard from a crash in the Penzendorfer Strasse, Schwabach, and Koellisch said that 3 were Canadian and 3 were English. (The aircraft was Lancaster I, PD275, and the seventh crew member, another Canadian, was captured by the Germans and became a Prisoner of War).[92] After their burial another English flyer was brought from a crash near Kammerstein. The other six crew members were taken prisoner, but the deceased [Jack] had crashed with the burning aircraft. All the papers belonging to these Airmen had been taken by the Luftwaffe authorities in Roth. They were the only aircraft to crash in this area on 16 March 1945, therefore the airman taken from the crash at Kammerstein must be Sgt Goldstein. Sgt Goldstein was buried with the other six airmen in a communal grave in the New Cemetery at Schwabach'".

SHALOM, JACK

"A letter dated 28 April 1947 from the Air Ministry to his immediate next-of-kin, reveals that an investigation on Sergeant Goldstein [Jack] was carried out by the Missing Search and Enquiry Service. According to their report Lancaster Mk1, Serial No. RF154, of No. 166 Squadron, (target Nuremburg) on board which Sgt Goldstein was an Air Gunner, crashed on 16 March 1945 at Kammerstein, Germany. One member of the crew, of which there was little doubt that it was Sgt Goldstein was found dead in the aircraft. The six other crew were captured by the Germans and became Prisoners of War, all later returning safely to the U.K in May 1945. It was later confirmed that the deceased airman was laid to rest in the New Cemetery, Schwabach, Allied Plot, Grave No. 1. He was later reburied in Bad Tolz, Durnbach British Military Cemetery, Plot IX, Row K, Grave 22"

"An Air Ministry letter on the Casualty file dated 8 September 1947 to Mrs S Goldstein, London, states that according to a report from the Missing Research & Enquiry service in Germany, it was definately[sic] established that Sergeant Goldstein was laid to rest in the New Cemetery, Schwabach, Allied Plot, Grave No. 1."

"An Air Ministry letter on the Casualty file dated 21 January 1949, and addressed to Mrs J Goldstein, London, states that a report had been received from the Missing Graves Registration Section, which stated that they had removed the grave of Sergeant J Goldstein to the British Military Cemetery at Bad Tolz, Durnbach, where he now rests in Grave No. 22, Row K, Plot XI."

The reference in the Air Ministry letter of 28 April 1947 to 'his immediate next-of-kin' is interesting. The image of Jack's Service Record Card obtained in around 1996 gives the next of kin as Sadie – with her name and address after her second marriage (which was from 1948); it can only be assumed that she would have been named as next of kin from the start, with her earlier address. However, the name of the 'Person to be Notified of Casualties' is Jack's eldest brother Lou. It is not clear if Sadie received this letter or if it went to Lou. But in any case, the other letters clearly set out the circumstances of the crash, and in particular:

"...crashed with the burning aircraft..."

"...was brought from a crash near Kammerstein..."

"...the airman taken from the crash..."

"...Sgt Goldstein was found dead in the aircraft..."

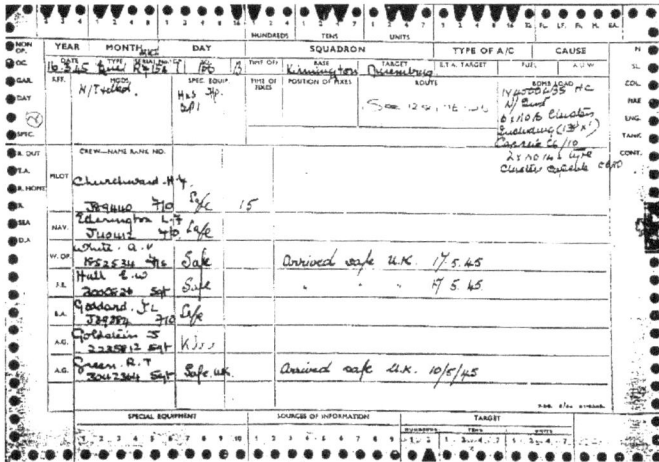

58 - Official report of the fate of the crew of RF154

There is, however an anomaly. The aircraft was seriously on fire as it fell from the sky, as the six 1000lb incendiaries had been set off by the shells of the fighter which brought the aircraft down. The 4000lb bomb had not been released when the aircraft was hit, and according to Ted Hull[7] the bomb doors were still closed, so the 'Cookie' would have still been in the bomb bay when falling to the ground; there would have been a huge explosion on impact. There were reports by other crews on the raid that night that the aircraft exploded before hitting the ground, with no chance of any of the crew still in the aircraft surviving; these reports are clearly now known to be erroneous. Jack crashed in the aircraft. Yet he did not suffer major burning, nor was his body destroyed. The exhumation report dated 24 June 1947, on Jack's reburial in the Commonwealth War Graves Cemetery in Dürnbach, Bavaria, describes his clothing and equipment as:

SHALOM, JACK

"Remains of RAF BD, Sgt's chevrons, airman issue shirt, long woollen underwear, blue aircrew sweater, blue aircrew socks, airman issue braces. Issue flying boots, escape type. Remains of mae west, and electrically heated flying suit".

59 - Report of exhumation of Jack's body, 24 June 1947

The fact that he was buried and re-buried in full flying gear is consistent with the body being very damaged, but nonetheless it is somewhat surprising that it was not torn apart by the explosion. Jack being buried in flying gear is further evidence that Ted was mistaken in thinking the prisoner he saw through his cell window was Jack, because he described that person as not being dressed in RAF uniform but in "the drab sort of garb" all the prisoners had on.

A 'Graves Concentration Report Form' completed 2 July 1948 identifies the six other airmen originally buried with Jack in Schwabach – crew of Lancaster I, PD275: P/O Malyon, F/O Kerr and F/Lt Daymond from RCAF; and Sgt Hathaway, P/O Woffenden and Sgt McNicol from RAFVR. Jack was described as 'Body 1' of seven. They were all reburied, in individual graves of course, on 18 June 1948 at the Commonwealth War Grave cemetery at Dürnbach, near Bad Töltz in Bavaria. This is the most southerly of all the Commonwealth War Graves in Germany and is about 45km south of Munich. Jack's grave identification is plot XI, row K, grave 22.

60 - Graves Concentration Report for reburial at Dürnbach of Jack and the six airmen of Lancaster PD275 killed the same night and originally buried with him in Schwabach New Cemetery

It was many years later that I obtained further eye-witness evidence of Jack's fate, as I shall describe later.

SHALOM, JACK

COPING WITHOUT JACK

It must have been the moment everyone dreaded...the knock on the door.... a policeman or a telegram boy….

It was Saturday 17 March 1945 when the policeman rang our doorbell. I recall seeing Sadie taking the telegram into the scullery, the only source of natural light in the tiny living area in 60 Fairholt Road. She kept her back to me, so I would not see her tears. I must have asked what was wrong, because she said (and although I was only just coming up to six years old at the time, I really do still remember the words, sixty years on): "Daddy's missing.... go out to play..."

Of course, I did. I wanted to tell my friends.

I did not really understand the trauma and significance of that dreadful message for a long time, but obviously it had deep and immediate impact on Sadie. In her own words, written on Armistice Day 1987, over 42 years after Jack's death:[10]

> "I could not accept what had happened. I kept telling myself that he would be found and placed in a prisoner of war camp, and eventually he would come home. I remember looking out of the window and watching the boys coming home to other families in the street, still hoping my door bell would ring. I am still waiting."

Years later, one of Jack's sisters, Debbie, gave me two well-folded and very worn letters which Sadie had written some weeks after that fateful day. They were addressed to Lou, the oldest of all the Goldstein boys, and with whom Sadie was very close. The first is dated Sunday 10 June (1945), over 12 weeks after the crash. Half of one of the three pages is missing, but the sense of the desperate hope, so long after Sadie received the telegram, still comes through. I have retained the punctuation etc as in the original. This is what it says:

> "Dear Lou,
>
> I am slipping this note to you in Dad's letter, as I feel I must tell you that there is now a little hope for Jack's safety.

SHALOM, JACK

I received a letter from Mrs Smith (the children, you remember, were billeted with her). She has a brother, a Ft/S, who is now stationed at Kirmington and knows Jack. Mrs Smith tells me that her brother has had 'secondhand' information that Jack is OK and is now back in this country since last Tues. from a P.O.W. camp.

So far I have had no official confirming this, but I went up to the Air Ministry on Friday, had an interview with a Flying Officer there and was told that only one.......[missing half-page]......plane. This is all I know at present, but I'm trying to contact Mrs Smith's brother at Kirmington and find out a little more.

If you have any spare time, write to the Air Ministry (Casualty Branch) 73-77 Oxford St W.1, and perhaps you can find out a little more about things.

Cheerio! then for now, hoping this finds you well,

all the best

Sadie"

The second letter was sent a few days later, on Tuesday 19 June 1945. It is less complete than the first one, but the messages are clear:

"Dear Lou,

I don't know whether you are still in England, but I hope you will eventually get this letter, so here goes.

On my visit to the Air Ministry yesterday, I learnt that all the crew, except Jack are now back in England and according to the P/O and W.O.P. Jack was killed by German ack-ack ground fire while baling out. The plane was hit and caught fire before even reaching the target and the crew eventually all met in the same P.O.W. camp in Germany, nothing was seen or heard of Jack while they were there.

I feel deep down inside me, that Jack is somewhere in hospital over there and I am still hoping and praying he is......

SHALOM, JACK

I have....the children....yet, in fact...

You...only one in....who has really...helpful during.....anxious period...I give you my heartfelt thanks and deepest gratitude.

Jack will always be alive in my heart and I'm sure in yours. Here's wishing you all the very best for the future....

....sincerely,

...."

There must have been countless thousands of families in this state; still praying; clinging on to hope of some mistake, some miracle.... I grew up with such secret hope, believing that one day my Dad would knock on the door again....

It is impossible to say how much the experiences I have related have really affected my character and outlook, but I like to think they have made me value human relations both in local environments and globally. War has always been an appalling waste in every conceivable sense, although it can also be justified, as in WW2. I was too young to be traumatised or damaged, but I know how much Sadie just hated the word. I know that when the first Gulf War began in 1990/91, she was physically ill about it. She never spoke to me or even Leila, who was five years older than me, about the wartime, or even about Jack; and I knew that she did not want to concern me about such matters. I guess it was her way of protecting me, and herself, from the sadness and hurt. She grieved all her life for her dear Jack and did not want me to grieve. The fact that we never spoke about Jack might seem odd to some, even sad. But it was our way of dealing with our distress.

Gradually, Sadie came to terms with the awful fact that Jack was dead. As referred to earlier, she received letters from the Air Ministry (dated 8 September 1947 and 21 January 1949) which represented the official confirmation. I have acquired a photograph of the temporary grave marker at Dürnbach, which is printed on 'Crown Copyright' photographic paper; it must have been sent to

SHALOM, JACK

Sadie. In due course, she received the Commemorative scroll sent to next-of-kin of those killed in World War 2, the text of which is:

"This scroll commemorates

Sergeant J. Goldstein

Royal Air Force

held in honour as one who served King and Country in the world war of 1939-1945 and gave his life to save mankind from tyranny. May his sacrifice help to bring the peace and freedom for which he died."

Later, she realised she had not automatically received Jack's medals, and had to go through considerable emotion to get them. They are:

The France and Germany Star

The War Medal 1939-45

The 1939-45 Star

Much later, in 2013, the Bomber Command clasp was added after a long public campaign to get recognition of Bomber Command service.

61 - Jack's medals. From left to right, they are: The 1939-1945 Star with Bomber Command Clasp; The France and Germany Star; The War Medal 1939-1945

But while at last realising that Jack had indeed been killed, she grieved for him all her life. A few years after being widowed for the second time, she wrote a letter to a newspaper or magazine (the cutting she left with her possessions does not identify the title or the date):

> "I read with interest (issue 34) Brian Gordon's comments ('Misplaced enthusiasm about Germany'). President Clinton is and always will be a warmonger, and, may I add, I am not an expert on politics. I'm just a broken-hearted widow, who suffered an unreplaceable loss in the last world war.
>
> Who was it that said, "Time is a healer"? That's just not true; as time goes by it becomes unbearable"

As Sadie began to accept that Jack was in the aircraft when it crashed, so she became bitter and angry at the rest of the crew – in her mind, they had abandoned him to die. She was distraught and angry that everyone else had survived and Jack had not. Ted Hull recalled to Ron, in his interview on 1 September 1996:

> "…I did write to [Sadie] and I'd arranged actually with Alf [White] and Bob Green that all three of us would go together. But probably because I didn't get in touch with her a soon as possible, Alf and Bob went to see her. And then when I felt not too bad again [after being in and out of hospital for treatment of war injuries] I wrote to Jack's widow and asked if I could go up and see her. Now I didn't tell you at the time what happened, but actually she wrote back, which to me at the time was a rather nasty letter implying that we got out and left Jack in there. She didn't say a word about going to see her, which upset me at the time, so much so that my father said, 'Shall I write to her?' and I said, 'Yes please' and I don't know any more or whether he wrote to her.
>
> "….I was rather nervous about what to say to her…. I understood that the poor woman was in a terrible state, obviously, but the idea of the three of us going together, I thought I can side-step any cross questioning as to what I'd seen. But I suppose in some sense when I didn't have to go up and see her that was probably a bit of relief.

> "…. [later] I didn't know where Jack's widow was. I heard she'd remarried….so I hadn't got a hope of finding her 'cos I didn't know what her new name was at the time, so it was very difficult. I didn't really do anything strenuous to find her."

The terrible news of the loss of Jack took some time to get to his brothers serving in the war. Lou was notified on 3 April 1945. Mick did not hear until 12 April 1945, when he was fighting in Italy. Ron received a letter giving the devastating news as he was sitting in a field near Venice with the tank earphones round his neck, listening to the crowds going mad with the news of VE Day, on 11 May 1945, having been relieved and believing his family had escaped the war unscathed.

Debbie recorded her feelings on hearing the news the her "darling brother" was, as reported in the telegram Sadie had received, "missing, presumed killed":[10]

> "I was shattered, but clung to the belief that he had escaped somehow and that he would return unharmed – after all, he was only 'presumed' killed. I started having a recurring dream – as I walked through Petticoat Lane market, with crowds of people milling around me, a few yards ahead I saw my brother Jack. I tried to get nearer to him and kept calling him, but he could not hear me, and the crowds separated us. That dream persisted, always the same, until the confirmation came from the War Office that my brother had been killed and was buried in a German cemetery; then they ceased, but the warm and loving memory of Jacky[37] remains with me forever."

Gertie wrote an article for a magazine[93] about how she found out about Jack, entitled "I'll Never Forget That Day." A shortened version of this account appears in her autobiography.[54] It is moving to the extent of bringing me to tears every time I read it:

> "It was early April 1945. Our enemies had been defeated. Thank God the War was drawing to a close.
> During those momentous years my large close family of siblings had been scattered, each of them living out their own wartime drama.

SHALOM, JACK

All five brothers, and five brothers-in-law, including my husband, had fought in the forces overseas, and all had mercifully come through, although not entirely unscathed.

On that day I'll never forget, I travelled up to London by train to meet my father for lunch, something we tried to do now and again, however difficult it was in those uncertain times. I noticed at once that he looked pale and ill, not at all his robust self.

To my horror he began to shake; his whole body shook, his face, his hands trembled.

Tears streamed down his cheeks as he told me in a broken voice that my beloved elder brother Jack, 33-year-old Sgt Air Gunner, had been shot down three weeks earlier in what proved to be the last air raid of the War over Germany,[94] and posted 'Missing, believed killed.' I asked shakily, 'Mum, does she know?' And my poor father faltered, a broken man, 'I can't tell her – I think she guesses, but I can't bring myself to tell her.'

I had no words with which to comfort him, and I had to return home to my little girl, my mind in turmoil.

Dazed with shock, I was torn with pity for Jack's young wife. Left with two children, a girl of ten and a boy of five. I found myself wandering the streets near Liverpool Street Station, reliving in my thoughts all the pain and hardship of my own wartime experiences. The bombing, the recent tragic loss of my baby son, my husband's wounding in Normandy. And now, at this eleventh hour, when we thought all our dear ones had survived, to be dealt this terrible blow!

We had all felt, as a family that our partings and privations had been for a worthy cause – now I asked myself, had it all been for nothing?

And then at that moment, like a miracle, I saw him, my brother Jack, across the street. How wonderful, it had all been some terrible mistake – he was alive – I was so happy as I raced across the road to tug at the sleeve of the slim

SHALOM, JACK

young man in airforce blue. I looked up into his face, laughing in my joy – and it wasn't him – it wasn't his face!

Embarrassed, heartbroken, confused, I stammered out my excuses. I was to suffer these fantasies for a long time, seeing my brother in every young man in uniform, having to stop myself running up to them.

Until the Red Cross located his grave, and we knew for sure that he was dead, shot while parachuting down from his burning plane.[95]

Jack lies buried in a War Cemetery near Dürnbach, where after the war our family members said *Kaddish*[96] over his grave with the *Magen Dovid*[97] on the headstone.

I end this story on a happier note.

Last month, in the 1997 Queen's Birthday Honours List, Jack's son, that fatherless little boy, Dr Michael Goldstein, now risen to the high rank in life of Vice Chancellor of Coventry University, was awarded the C.B.E. for his service to the Higher Education. Michael is a great, yet modest man. His sister Leila is a dedicated social worker who cares lovingly for her now ailing mother.

Jack – your sacrifice was not in vain. You did not grow old as we who are left grow old, but your noble spirit lives on in the lives of your children.

This is my tribute to your memory."

My cousin Laurence Rosen, elder son of Jack's sister Esther (the first sibling to be born in England), told me that Esther "mourned Jack's passing for many, many years, tears often in her eyes as she talked about him as the clever and creative brother and the quietly ambitious one," and describing Jack as "her soulmate in the family, smart as paint and strong-willed."

The period after Sadie got the news that her Jack was missing, later confirmed as killed, must have been incredibly traumatic for her. We two children were a handful — I was not yet six, and my sister Leila was just coming up to eleven years old. Knowing that Jack would never come home again meant that she had to shoulder the responsibility of their family alone. It was to be about three years before she would marry again.... three years to bear the responsibility of bringing up two children by herself.[98]

We had no money to fall back on, so times were very hard indeed. Sadie's war widow's pension was meagre. Pensions varied hugely according to the rank of the serviceman killed. By 1944 it was set at a minimum of 32/- (£1.60) a week, with 11/- (55p) a week for each child. War widows were expected to work and not be dependent on the State, so the pension was regarded as 'unearned income' and taxed at 50%. The pension was withdrawn from war widows found to be co-habiting. It is hard now to believe how women who had lost their husbands fighting for their country could be so poorly treated. There were many other issues and anomalies too, and it took years of campaigning to get the changes which were needed for just and fair treatment of all war widows.[98]

Obviously, then, Sadie's war widow's pension did not provide sufficient for her and her two young children. Neither Sadie's nor Jack's family was able to help financially, but they provided support in several ways. The most important materially was that Sadie was able to work in the Goldstein family's clothing factory. She was a self-taught whizz with the needle, and this provided the means for her to have an income.

Sadie going to work meant, of course, that Leila and I had to fend for ourselves for a while after school before Sadie could get home from the factory in London's East End. As I have previously described, the landlord of the house in which we rented three rooms would not allow us to have keys to the house, and neither were we allowed to use the garden, so we played in the street in all weathers, waiting for Mum to get home. It was quite safe to do so in those days. There were few cars driving along our streets - I didn't even know anyone who had one - and we were oblivious to any of the nasty and evil things which seem to dominate young parents' concerns these days. We amused ourselves playing with an old tin can, a box or a ball - I remember we used the 'pig bin' (into which everyone was encouraged to put their food scraps for collection and transporting out to farms, during and just after war-time) as a cricket wicket. Skipping was a regular bit of fun and exercise - for the boys too. We also spent ages playing 'buses' on a long garden wall. In the Spring we collected butterflies. The cold weather of winter didn't seem to bother us, and certainly when the extremes of the famous 1946/7 winter came, we made the most of playing in the snow. The 1948 Olympics, held in London, were a stimulus to organise our own races round the block. What with collecting conkers and having our own conker championships, plus a bit of scrumping, we managed to pass the time in pretty creative ways.

But, as I said, family support was important too. All my uncles and aunts, on both sides of the family, had their problems after the war, and struggled to re-build their lives. But I particularly remember my uncle Ron Goldstein, trying to fill the huge gap which Jack's death had left in the lives of Leila and me. Our fondest memory is of him taking us to Madam Tussaud's waxworks in Baker Street — what an amazing experience that was for us! And the fantastic luxury of having tea in Lyons Corner House in the West End — sitting at a table with a crisp white tablecloth, served by smart waitresses in frilly uniforms, and with someone playing a grand piano just a few yards away. And the wonderful memory of the dessert — 'Apple Foam and Melba Sauce.' How that thought often comes back to me and makes my mouth water! And it was Ron to whom Sadie turned when I needed long trousers and a trilby hat to appear as a juror in the Montefiore House School production of Gilbert and Sullivan's 'Trial by Jury'. And who else but Ron would be called upon to help the little lad learn how to ride a bike?

The school holidays were a particular problem, with Mum at work. Leila remembers that we were sent one year to stay in Frittendon, near Chatteris in Cambridgeshire, and indeed the name Chatteris rings a bell in my memory too. But my better recollection is being sent to a farm in Kent for two successive summers. I can even see the layout of the farmhouse with the fields and wood vaguely in my mind's eye. The family had a son - I think his name was Colin — and I recall that Leila, who was 12-13 by then, had a crush on him. As a young lad brought up in Stamford Hill, London, I found the very nature of a farm hugely alien to me. It isn't surprising that I had some memorable experiences there - like crossing the (very deep) pond in a barrel; sleeping all night with Colin in a (poorly) cleaned-out pig sty; walking in the woods which were full of huge rhododendron bushes in full bloom (having hardly seen any flowers before then); and finding grass snakes.

I also spent a week or so one summer in the outskirts of Southampton. Sadie was friendly with a Mrs Ellis who worked in the United Dairies shop in Dunsmure Road, just a few minutes' walk from our house in Fairholt Road. There was a small parade of shops there where we did most of our shopping (apart from the weekly trek to the famous Ridley Road market). Mrs Ellis had a sister who had moved out of London to a new estate on the edge of Southampton and offered to take me there for a holiday. Her sister had a son about my age and it seemed a good opportunity for me to get a short holiday. I remember that Mr and Mrs Ellis had a motorbike and sidecar, and I had to travel in the side-car rather than be the pillion passenger, much to my disappointment! We had some good adventures that week. I still have the penny (1d) coin which is about 50% larger than normal after I left it to be splayed by a passing train speeding along the open railway line that was near the back of the estate.

I also have some recollections of going to an RAF base in Bungay in Suffolk — why else would I have the name of such a place so firmly planted in my memory? I can visualise myself in the back of a Land-Rover speeding through country lanes, holding on in excited fear; and getting up early one morning to go with some men with shotguns to shoot rabbits — but coming back with a pigeon instead.

But somehow, we came through all that hardship and trauma. In 1947 someone new came into our lives, as Sadie met and then married Alf (Aaron) Hyman. It was clearly very difficult for Leila and me to adjust, and I confess not to have been the most adaptable at first. It did not help that early on Alf bought me a book and wrote inside: "To Mick. Be a good boy and there will be more on the way." For a start, I did not like being called 'Mick' – from then on I hated it, and still do. And although I was only eight years old I was savvy enough to understand the bribe. I cannot recall anything about the book– I doubt I even read it - other than the damning inscription. To be fair, Alf didn't stand much chance of winning me over. But it was evident to me that Sadie was securing her children's future, and Leila and I realised that this new phase in our lives was all for the better. So it proved, although at times the marriage was fractious, for example, the time Sadie agreed I could buy a pet mouse, and Alf did not….

At the time, Leila, aged 13, was not only sharing the same bedroom as me, aged eight, but also the same bed, as there was no space for separate ones. Sadie nagged to submission a local Councillor who lived nearby to get us a Council flat, and so we moved to 24 Binyon House, Milton Grove, in a new block of flats a couple of miles away at the other end of Stoke Newington, near Newington Green. The development was newly-built after the war and was described as 'luxury flats' – which they most certainly were not! But for the first time Sadie had her own front door and bathroom, something she had dreamt of with Jack, some 14 years earlier.

David was born a short while later, on 27 January 1949. And the rest, as they say, is history.....

SHALOM, JACK

THE OTHERS

After the six surviving member of the crew of RF154 were returned to England, the three Canadians ('Bud' Churchward, 'Chuck' Goddard, and 'Lefty' Etherington) returned to Canada and continued their interrupted lives.

I had some correspondence with Bud's grandson (son of Bud's daughter, Patricia), Mike Murphy, towards the end of 2011. He had seen Ron's stories of Jack on the internet and made contact to find out more about his grandfather's wartime experiences. Like many ex-service people, Bud did not speak much, if at all, about those times. He told me that Bud had passed away in 2005.

According to Alf White (from his interview with Ron on 29 April 1997), Chuck Goddard was killed in a road accident in Canada "some time after the war."

Lefty Etherington's son made contact in 2015. His name is Jack, and it is almost certain that he was named after Jack Goldstein. That was quite something for me! He told me that Lefty died in 2002, aged 78.

Bob Green emigrated to Canada after the war and joined the Royal Canadian Mounted Police (RCMP). He remained good friends with Lefty Etherington and maintained close contact with him. He died of cancer shortly before retiring from the RCMP.

Ted Hull renewed his life with Betty in a sleepy Worcestershire village, Martin Hussingtree, where I visited on a couple of occasions, as did my sister, Leila. He passed away in June 2001, and Betty, his wife, in July 2011.

The Lancaster from 12 Squadron, PD275, has a special place in Jack's story. This was the Lancaster on the Nürnberg raid that crashed not far from Jack's crash – in a garden between house numbers 67 and 69 Penzendorfer Strasse, Schwabach. In addition to six of the crew, sadly, 9 civilians were also killed, including three children - four instantly, the other five succumbing to their injuries over the next few days.[99] One member of the crew, James H Clarke (known as 'Jim') bailed out and was soon captured. He returned safely to Canada after being liberated. The other six crew members:

    Pilot – Fl/Lt Keith William Daymond, RCAF

    Engineer – Sgt Arthur William Hathaway, RAFVR

    Navigator – F/O Bertram Clarence Kerr, RCAF

    Wireless Op/Gunner – P/O William John Malyon, RCAF

    Air Gunner – P/O Harry Woffenden, RAFVR

    Air Gunner – Sgt Neil McNicol, RAFVR

were all killed and buried in a communal grave in Schwabach with Jack, until re-internment in Dürnbach. The details were researched by Linda Ibrom and recorded on the website of the Aircrew Remembrance Society.[100]

62 - Photographs taken by a local resident of the site of the crash of PD275 from 12 Squadron in which six of the seven-man crew were killed, as were nine civilians on the ground at Schwabach, 16 March 1945

SHALOM, JACK

In April 2014, I had a surprise telephone call from a Paul Clarke, who said he was Jim Clarke's son, and we spent over an hour in conversation, comparing notes and stories. This is some of what he later wrote to me:

> "My father, James H ('Jim') Clarke, signed up for service with the RCAF in late 1941. He progressed through training at several Air Observer Schools, Bombing and Gunnery School, etc. He received his commission as an officer in December 1942. He was chosen to be an instructor in bombing. He was posted to a Bombing and Gunnery School in Saskatchewan, where he spent over a year training new recruits from across the Commonwealth. Finally, anxious to serve in the action, he was posted overseas in February 1944.
>
> The usual sequence of training for Bomber Command then followed, through Advanced Flying Unit, Operational Training Unit, Heavy Conversion Unit, and Lancaster Finishing School. Posting to the RAF's 12 Squadron, Wickenby, occurred in October 1944. He was the Bombardier/back-up Navigator of his crew.
>
> I note an item that may be of some significance to you from his flying log book. At No. 2 AFU Millom, Cumberland, he records a training flight on April 10/44 in an Anson with him as Air Bomber and with a Flight/Sergeant Goldstein as the Pilot! Is this a relative of yours?
>
> When he took off on the night of March 16, 1945, Dad did not know that his promotion to Flight Lieutenant had come through. In fact, it was granted with effect from December 18, 1944, but I understand that delays in notification were quite frequent, especially for RCAF serving with squadrons of other forces."

The reference to a 'Goldstein' is interesting but no more than coincidental, because Jack was not a Pilot and was not stationed at RAF Millom.

Paul attached his father's story of his experience in the fateful Nürnberg raid of 16 March 1945, his 26th and last operation. It was written in Jim's log book in September 1945 after his return to Canada, and so was a relatively fresh account. The story was published in the Royal Canadian Air Force City of Toronto Wing 408 Year Book for 1953, as a slightly abridged version of the log book entry. His account is another harrowing story of great bravery and tragedy for so many. When his Pilot gave the order to abandon the aircraft he already had on his parachute and was able to jump out quite quickly. He could feel the Engineer, who also had on his parachute, and who was second in line of the front crew members to jump, coming behind him to the hatch. But sadly, the aircraft must have exploded just before the Engineer (and the others) was able to bail out, as all were killed. Jim landed in a clump of trees near a house, and apparently turned over and hit his head on the ground. He must have passed out because the next he knew he was awakened by police, called by the house owner, poking him in the ribs and covering him with a gun. He remained a prisoner of war until liberation.

Early in November 2011 I received a telephone call from someone who was quite well known to me, Geoffrey Alderman, who was then Michael Gross Professor of Politics & Contemporary History at the University of Buckingham (since 2014 he has been Principal of Nelson College London). Like me, he went to Hackney Downs Grammar School, although a few years after me. He had read my BBC WW2 People's War accounts of Jack,[8] and the my partial autobiography in the book written with an aunt and niece,[11] and wondered if his uncle, Sgt Henry Landau, who was also killed in action serving in 166 Squadron, had ever met Jack. I checked the 166 Squadron Roll of Honour,[101] which gives the date of death of Geoffrey's uncle as 22 January 1944. I was astonished at the coincidence, as that is the date of the first entry in Jack's service record when he was posted to Euston/3ACRC – Number 3 Aircrew Reception Centre. So while they could never have met, they have that date in common, albeit with opposing effects – Henry Landau being killed on the exact same day Jack enlisted!

SHALOM, JACK

DŰRNBACH[102]

The Commonwealth War Graves Commission cemetery at Dürnbach is near the small village of Dürnbach, which lies in the south of Germany approximately 45km south of Munich. The cemetery address is Am Moos 83703 Gmund am Tegernsee Germany GPS Location is N 47° 46' 42" E 11° 44' 0.7" The site for Dürnbach War Cemetery was chosen, shortly after hostilities had ceased, by officers of the British Army and Air Force, in conjunction with officers of the American Occupation Forces in whose zone Dürnbach lay. The great majority of those buried here are airmen shot down over Bavaria, Wurtemberg, Austria, Hessen and Thuringia, brought from their scattered graves by the Army Graves Service. The remainder are men who were killed while escaping from prisoner of war camps in the same areas, or who died towards the end of the War on forced marches from the camps to more remote areas.

Dürnbach war cemetery contains 2,934 Commonwealth burials of the Second World War, 93 of which are unidentified. One grave in the cemetery (III. C. 22.) contains the ashes of an unknown number of unidentified war casualties recovered from Flossenburg. Also, one grave (IV. A. 21.) contains the remains of six unidentified U.K. airmen. There are also 30 war graves of other nationalities, most of them Polish. Within the Indian section of the cemetery there is the Dürnbach cremation memorial, commemorating 23 servicemen of the army of undivided India who died while prisoners of war in various places in France and Germany, and who were cremated in accordance with their religion.

According to some locals, the reason for locating the cemetery in such a remote location is an affront to the fact that *Reichsführer* Heinrich Himmler and his family maintained a home at Gmund am Tegernsee from 1934, and that Bad Tölz was the SS Headquarters. It was thus a way to make sure that local people did not forget some of what happened in WW2.

It has always been a mystery to me how it was that some of Jack's siblings first visited his grave in Dürnbach without Sadie. I am not even sure she knew they were going. The fact they visited is recorded[10] by Esther, who says she, her husband Jack together with Debbie and her husband Alec:

> "….stood beside his grave in Germany in the military cemetery not far from Munich and said our prayers."

Gertie relates:[54]

> "Years later [after the war], our family stood round his grave in a war cemetery near Munich and said the Jewish prayers for the dead – the *Kaddish*[96] – for him."

63 - Jack's temporary grave marker at Dürnbach War Graves Cemetery

Gertie's use of the term 'our family' implies she was not herself present, which accords with Esther's account. But I am not convinced Sadie knew anything about this. Certainly, I was later to find out that she had independently tried to locate Jack's grave. The story of this is worthy of some description.

It was 1956. I was in the sixth-form at Hackney Downs Grammar School and had just taken my A-level examinations in Chemistry, Physics, Pure Mathematics and Applied Mathematics. I was only 17 as I had accelerated a year at school, so I was a year ahead of the norm. I was wondering what I was going to do in the summer while I waited for the examination results and my applications to get in to a College of London University. If nothing else came up I would work in True-Form, where I had a part-time job since the age of 16, working every Saturday and school holidays so as to be as financially independent as I could, and not be a burden on the very meagre household budget. A fellow sixth-former, Brian Levy (known as 'Levy B R' to distinguish him from the other Levy in the class, 'Levy L') was asking around if anyone wanted to hitch-hike round Europe with him. I did not really know him at all well and had never hitch-hiked anywhere in England, let alone abroad, but I rarely had a holiday as such, so decided to go with him. I was very surprised Sadie agreed I could go, as I was anything but adventurous or outward-going. Anyhow, we made our preparations and off we went.

I had a return train ticket from London to Calais and just £20 in my pocket to last me for four weeks (food, hostel fees, travel and all); rucksack on the back, Union Jack sewn on top to encourage cars to stop for us, map in hand, and (Sadie's insistence!) plenty of spare socks... Our journey was to take us from our port of entry through Belgium and Holland, into Germany and Austria, across northern Italy into southern France and Switzerland, and then back north via Paris to the French coast. It was an experience never to be forgotten.... There is much to tell about that, but the only point relevant here is that amongst the many hitch-hikers we met on our travels was a young German student called Lothar Eichhoff. He was a few years older than me, at a University in West Berlin, his home town. Brian and I were somewhere in central Germany, trying to make our way to Italy. In those days there were plenty of young people, generally students, hitch-hiking (or '*Autostopfahren*' as the Germans would say) across the continent. We were standing at the end of a link road to an *Autobahn* (motorway) – walking on the *Autobahn* was strictly forbidden, as it is in the UK now we have motorways – when a car stopped for us. We were getting in when I heard from behind me a voice "*Darf Ich aus mitfahren?'* ['May I also travel with you?']. There was room, and the driver agreed to take all of us. Later that evening we met at the same *Jugendherberge* [youth hostel] and became quite friendly. We exchanged addresses and telephone numbers, particularly because Lothar said he would like to look me up during his trip to England on a spell of fruit-picking later that summer. I thought little of him after returning to England, but a few weeks later he telephoned me to say he would be calling in at our London home on his way back to Germany at the end of his working holiday in Wisbech, Cambridgeshire. When I asked Sadie if it was alright for Lothar to come, I was surprised that she was so clearly in favour, because I knew she was still very bitter about the war, and not forgiving to Germany or Germans in any sense. But when Lothar arrived at our Council flat in Stoke Newington she was very friendly, and spoke to him in Yiddish, which was close enough to German for him to understand.

It was some months later that I received a letter from Lothar (dated 16 January 1957), which I still have, telling me about his journey back to Germany (he lived in West Berlin) and something about his life there. It was a very pleasant letter, but I was astonished to read that he told me had also written to Sadie about 'that war grave cemetery in Germany.' It seemed that when Lothar was with us, and completely unbeknown to me, Sadie had asked him to help locate Jack's grave. She clearly knew the name and address of the cemetery in which Jack was buried from letters she had received years earlier from the Air Ministry, but she had asked Lothar to find out more details. As was later apparent, she wanted to visit. Indeed, two years earlier she had written to the Imperial War Graves Commission (later re-named the Commonwealth War Graves Commission) asking about visiting and seeking a photograph of the grave. The reply from the IWGC, dated 3 March 1955, is as follows:

> "Dear Madam,
> Thank you for your letter of 28th February in respect of the grave of the late Sergeant J. Goldstein.
> I regret that the Commission are unable to supply photographs of graves as this is not part of their duty. The British Legion, 49 Pall Mall, London, S.W.1 have a service whereby these may be obtained at a reasonable charge, and if you would write to them they would be able to assist you. In writing to the Legion, you should quote the full name and service particulars, as under:-
>
> 2235812 Sergeant J. Goldstein,
> Royal Air Force,
> Durnbach War Cemetery, Germany,
> Plot XI, Row K, Grave No. 22.

> I very much regret that the Commission do not make arrangements for visits to war graves overseas neither are they able to grant any financial assistance to relatives for this purpose. The British Legion arrange visits from time to time and I can only suggest that you write to them in this matter.
> Yours faithfully,
> N Dean
> Secretary"

I do not know whether Sadie followed up on these suggestions, but it does explain her request to Lothar, whose postcard reply was sent on the same day as his letter to me (16 January 1957):

> "Dear Mrs Hyman [Sadie's surname following her re-marriage in 1948],
>
> Probably you think I have forgotten you at all. But I hope you will not resent of me, that I write so late only. In the first days of November I tried to find out the real situation of that War Cemetery, attending some offices in Berlin, But no success. They didn't know anything about it. At last I got another address of a central office for <u>German</u> War Graves in Western Germany. In the beginning of December wrote to them. Last week I got the answer and I shall write you about it now: In German the villiage (sic) is written 'Dürnbach.' Official address: Dürnbach, Kreis Meisenbach/Bayern. Dürnbach is situated near the lake 'Tegernsee,' which is in the South of Munich. If you have any questions left, please write it to me. All the best in the new year I wish to you and your family.
>
> Lothar Eichhoff"

There is a small sketch showing Tegernsee (a lake) 'about 30 miles' south of Munich, and a PS:

> "Once more many thanks for your hospitality. Often I remember of these days."

I do not recall Sadie and I talking about this at all, and I guessed the matter had been quietly dropped. But I was wrong, because several years later in early 1979, when Janet (my first wife) and I were visiting Sadie and Alf, she dropped a bombshell.... they were planning to visit Jack's grave. Janet and I just looked at each other.... We both knew that they had no real idea what was involved. They had hardly been outside London, let alone abroad! We just couldn't see how they would ever get there, let alone manage with passports, language, travel, currency and all the rest. It didn't take long for us to decide: we would take them.

We decided to make a family holiday of it that summer — not that it was the kind of trip of itself to be viewed as a holiday, but that was a way to take away some of the drama, and to share the experience in a broader way. We would go by car, take a few days to get there and likewise on the return journey, and stay at a holiday resort where Janet, our son Richard and I had previously stayed — Seefeld in the Tyrol, Austria.

Having travelled down to London from our Sheffield home, we stayed overnight before setting off early the next day, on Tuesday 24 July 1979. I knew that Sadie in particular had no sense of distance, and that she would need frequent stops on the way, so about half-an-hour out of Calais I pulled over into a lay-by to pour out some tea from the vacuum flasks we had prepared for the trip. 'Are we nearly there?' came mother's voice from the back. When we recovered from our laughter, we explained (again) that the journey would take three days, and that we had booked rooms on the way....

It was a very eventful trip to Seefeld. We had lots of laughs and good humour on the way.... but I must not dwell on that aspect. After a few days in Seefeld, we decided that the day had come to find the cemetery. But my mother was not well that day. She had an upset stomach again and could not keep food down. This was not new — she had been unwell for some years and had been in and out of hospital trying to find out the reason for her discomfort and sickness. They had taken out her gall bladder, her appendix, and God knows what else, all to no effect. On this occasion we thought her upset stomach was simply due to nerves. It was not until a few years later, that we discovered she was a coeliac, allergic to gluten in wheat products, a complaint that was barely heard of in those

SHALOM, JACK

days. The problem that day in Seefeld was that having had continental breakfast with a couple of rolls every morning was just about the last thing she should have eaten. But we had to fulfil the purpose of the trip, so off we went that day.

Our instructions were not perfect. This was the time before satellite navigation and the internet, of course, and we were relying on an address and a not-as-good-as-we-thought map! It didn't take long for us to get lost. My German was not too bad in those days, which helped. A kindly old man in the country directed us to a small clearing by the roadside. We climbed the bank, through a gap in a hedge, to a cemetery....it was overgrown, uncared for, neglected, and anonymous. Our hearts sank. Was this the last resting place of our dearly loved husband and father? Had we come all this way only to find that the burial ground was a forgotten wilderness? His memory was filling our heads and our hearts that day, not forgotten! I thought: 'How could I have let this happen? I wish we had never come...' And then it dawned on me as I pulled away the weeds and read the headstones — this was a <u>German</u> cemetery, not the one we were looking for! Such relief, tinged with embarrassment that I had got it so wrong....

An hour or so later, and all this heartbreak was forgotten. We came across the most wonderful cemetery we had ever seen. It was a beautiful place, miles from nowhere, all alone. So clean, so well kept.... there were two gardeners busying away all the time we were there. The sun was shining, the breeze relaxing. It was so peaceful, so emotional. We found the actual plot and gravestone, and huge feelings swelled up inside each and every one of us. The little tears at the corners of our eyes; we kept control to a degree. We each walked around the cemetery, together and alone with our personal thoughts, shedding our tears in private.... reading the countless gravestones. In the entrance porch was the book of remembrance. There was my father's name. More emotions, more tears. We walked some more round that wonderful and serene pace. The huge stone memorial, inscribed in those compelling words: 'THEIR NAME LIVETH FOR EVERMORE'. More lumps in throats, more tears. We took many photographs, from every angle possible. Then it was time to go. We were all exhausted with emotion. We went through the gatehouse again and recorded our visit in the Book of

SHALOM, JACK

Remembrance. It was there that Sadie wrote just one simple word, which has been reflected also in the title of this book - 'Shalom' - against the location of Jack's grave. My emotions welled up again. I knew one thing: I had to come back!

The journey back to Seefeld was quiet. We each held our own comfort, had our own thoughts. But we knew it had been a wonderful and uplifting experience for us all. It was probably the most emotional period in my life. I couldn't believe I had left it so long before going there. I would have to go back again soon. We were so glad we had made it happen for Sadie. It was for her a dream fulfilled; in a way, a pilgrimage achieved.

64 - Entrance Lodge at Dürnbach, containing the Register and Book of Remembrance

65 - Pergola and rest-shelter at Dürnbach

66 – Jack's gravestone is in the centre of view

67 - Jack's gravestone. Dedication is:
FOR EVER REMEMBERED
WIFE SADIE CHILDREN
LEILA AND MICHAEL
PARENTS AND FAMILY

68 – 'Their Name Liveth For Evermore' is a promise fulfilled

SHALOM, JACK

The next few days in and around Seefeld were holiday, and we were more relaxed than on the first few days. We enjoyed ourselves and had some fun. I guess the ending of the tensions, the feeling of being fulfilled, made for a very pleasant time. There were some funny incidents — like when we were walking through the main square of Innsbruck and a small dog jumped out from under a table and bit my son Richard's leg — he was wearing shorts — breaking the skin. '*Der Hund hat bissen der Kind!*' shrieked my mother spontaneously in Yiddish ['The dog has bitten the child!'] — the poor elderly gentleman owner didn't know what to say as she waded into him.... Fortunately, as we found when we rushed back to Seefeld to see a doctor, there was no rabies in Austria....

Not long after our return, Sadie wrote a letter entitled 'Fulfilling a dream' to the *Jewish Chronicle*, published on 24 August 1979; and a very similar one entitled 'Visit to war cemetery realised a family dream' to her local newspaper, *The Hackney and Kingsland Gazette*, published on 17 August 1979:

> "Everyone has their dreams and disappointments through life, but our family has nursed a dream for a long time. For more than 30 years we have ached in the heart to discover the resting place of my first husband, Jack, so cruelly taken from us on 16 March 1945.
>
> In pursuit of this dream, we left England on Tuesday 24 July, drove to Dover and across by Seaspeed to Calais, through France and on to Germany. Our destination, the Commonwealth War Cemetery, which is situated outside the remote village of Dürnbach, where our loved one is buried. This is one of the lesser known war cemeteries and is not easily located. However, we finally found this signposted. Our feelings as we drove towards the entrance were indescribable, as were our emotions, and we stood and gazed in awe at the sight of row upon row of headstones among beds of flowers, with barely a blade of grass out of place.
>
> We checked the Visitors' Book and found the details of grave and row, number and name that we required. As we

read some of the inscriptions on the headstones we began to realise that the night of 16/17 March 1945 had indeed been a busy, operational and fateful one for our fallen airmen.

We discovered too a plot of graves set aside for Indian servicemen and began to wonder whether any of their relatives had visited the cemetery some time. The peace and tranquillity within the cemetery, with the Austrian Alps in the background must be seen to be believed.

When we took a last look back and said *'Shalom'* we drove away, realising a dream had, at long last, become a reality. Now we are at peace with the world knowing our loved one is resting peacefully in a world far removed from the agonies of those not-forgotten war days.

We would be very interested to hear whether any of your readers have visited this particular cemetery.

Sadie Hyman (formerly Goldstein)"

I have returned to Dürnbach several times since. It still retains for me a magical effect. Tears still flow, unashamedly when I am there, and even when I simply think of the experience of being there. Thank God for that place.

My visit in April 2012 was particularly poignant. After my previous visit in 2008, my niece Lynn (Leila's younger daughter) said she would like to go with me on the next occasion. Around the same time, I had a similar request from Ron Goldstein. I asked my sister, Leila, if she would like to go, and so the party became Lynn, Leila, Ron and his wife Nita, and me.

We decided to meet at Munich Airport on Tuesday 24 April 2012. I travelled from Birmingham Airport; Leila, Ron and Nita flew from Stanstead; and Lynn from Heathrow. We met just after 11am, in the arrivals hall at Munich Airport, collected a large people-carrier and made our way to Bad Tölz, where we had reserved rooms at *Hotel am Wald*. Our journey was fortunately uneventful, except that as we drove to higher ground it began to snow and we had to cope with a blizzard! Fortunately, this did not last. We had the rest of the day to relax and sight-see, before enjoying a lovely evening meal together. The following day, Wednesday 25 April (co-incidentally Leila's 78th birthday), we made our way to the cemetery, some seven miles distant.

69 - Group visit to Dürnbach 2012. From left to right: Leila, Lynn, me, Ron, and Nita

70 - Ron in discussion with Paul Willing, Head Gardener at Dürnbach War Graves Cemetery

It was a beautiful day with the temperature reaching a very pleasant 20° - after the snow of the previous day We soon reached our destination and were immediately overtaken by the same emotions I always get when I go to Dürnbach. For all of us, it was a very moving occasion. Ron and I stood in front of Jack's grave and said *Kaddish*[96] and *El Maleh Rachamim*.[103] We left small stones on top of the gravestone, the traditional ritual when visiting a Jewish grave.[104] We walked around the cemetery, deep within ourselves but also sharing emotions. Ron had a list of 19 graves of Jewish servicemen he wanted to photograph for the Association of Jewish Ex-Servicemen and Women (AJEX), seeking to record all such graves, as well as two others whose personal requests he had solicited via the ww2talk.com forum to which he was a frequent and long-standing contributor. We spoke to the Head Gardener, Paul Willing, and his wife. He was from South Africa and she was German, and they had made their life in the area. Paul was amazing. He was not just the gardener. He had researched the people who were buried there and regarded them as his friends. He referred to everyone buried there as 'gentleman,' and was so knowledgeable it was breath-taking. He told us so many stories about how they had

SHALOM, JACK

been killed, He was a remarkable man, and so keen to share his knowledge with us.

One example of what Paul Willing told us was the mystery of 'Operation Whiskey,' the last flight of Halifax V9976 of 138 Squadron on 20 April 1942. Curiously, there are few records of this mission, but it is known that the normal Pilot of V9976 was replaced by none other than the commander of RAF Tempsford, Wing Commander W R Farley, whose capture would have had disastrous security and secrets consequences; clearly this was an extremely important mission for Farley to have piloted it. It is believed the assignment was for the Soviet Secret Service with the support of the British Special Operations Executive. The aircraft mysteriously crashed into the Blauberg mountains in the Bavarian Alps just above Tegernsee. It is suggested that its target was Jenbach in the Austrian Tyrol, which was then the headquarters of Heinkel, one of Germany's high-tech armaments centres, and where an old mine had been turned into a secret aircraft factory in which V2 components were later built. This was a very secret mission, and there are further rumours about it.[105] All eight crew members were killed on that mission and are buried in Dürnbach cemetery.

We told Paul more about Jack, and there was no doubt that he logged it all in his future repartee for other visitors. Here was someone who cared about this job like no-one else I have ever met. I felt he was a new-found friend of my father, Jack.

We left after about two hours there, much more elated than when we had arrived; and content that our mission had been well and truly fulfilled.

We spent the rest of the day as tourist – visiting Gmund and walking round the beautiful lake of Tegernsee, before heading back for a last stroll round the charming town of Bad Tölz and returning to the hotel for dinner.

Lynn had to leave the hotel by taxi at 4am the next day to catch her 7.20am departure from Munich Airport, but the rest of us had the day free for further tourism, which we used well. We ate and drank local food, wines and beer, and basked in the Spring sunshine, reflecting all the time, inwardly and in conversation, on the fulfilment of the purpose and significance of the trip. With much satisfaction, we left Munich on our respective flights just after 9pm, and all returned safely home before the day was gone.

I found out after our return, that Ron and Nita had serious misgivings about going. They did not feel they could ever, emotionally, go to Germany, given the atrocities committed by the German people on Jews; it was a deep resentment which they struggled to contain. But their desire to visit Jack's grave was compelling, and they managed to supress their negativity remarkably. In the event, they realised that modern Germany is hugely different to the time of the Nazis. They formed a warm feeling about Germany and the Germans we met, and were able really to appreciate the trip. That was the added bonus for me - being happy that I was able to share the experience of visiting Jack's grave with my sister Leila, her daughter Lynn, and my dear uncle Ron and aunt Nita – two wonderful people who had been so significant in shaping my life.

Lynn is an award-winning freelance documentary filmmaker. She has had many great successes, specialising in 'fly-on-the-wall' documentaries with a difference.[106] She was so taken by her time at Dürnbach cemetery, and in particular with the personal way in which Paul Willing went way beyond his role as gardener. She decided this could be the subject of a short film, portraying the cemetery as a community of Paul's 'gentlemen friends.'

Lynn returned to Dürnbach later that year and learned of a remarkable annual event commemorating the war dead from both German and Allied forces. The 'Act of Remembrance' in Gmund and Dürnbach is jointly organised by the Commonwealth War Graves Commission (CWGC) and the equivalent German organisation, *Volksbund* (full name, *Volksbund Deutsche Kriegsgräberfürsorge,* [Commission for the Care of German War Graves]). It takes place on 11 November every year, a week after the German national day of mourning, *Volkstrauertag,* and coinciding with Armistice Day as commemorated in the UK and Commonwealth. It begins with a ceremony in Gmund, at the *Soldatenfreidhof Gmund* [Gmund Military Cemetery], attended by the British Consul General, the Mayor of Gmund, Bavarian officials and other dignitaries. Both German and British flags are raised, and

SHALOM, JACK

both national anthems are sung. After prayers and readings, there are speeches of commemoration by the British Consul General (in German) and a German State dignitary (in English), followed by wreath-laying ceremonies by them and Consular officials from Hungary, Croatia, France and Canada, as well as by the RAF. Finally, after the firing of a rifle-salute, the Bavarian, national German, and British anthems are sung.

71 - Dignitaries, servicemen and women, and members of the public join in the Remembrance Day Ceremony at Dürnbach War Graves Cemetery

72 - Servicemen from several nations join in the Dürnbach Ceremony

73 - Wreaths from several nations around the central cross

74 - The final tribute

SHALOM, JACK

The procession, including about 50-60 from the *Gebirgsschützenkompanie Gmund* [Gmund Mountain Rifle Brigade], then marches ceremoniously to the CWGC Cemetery of Dürnbach. Both flags are again raised, the military band plays, and the Chaplain begins the service of commemoration, largely in the style of the countless Remembrance Day services held across the UK – recitation of 'Going Down of the Sun,' a sole trumpeter playing The Last Post, a two-minutes silence, and the trumpeter playing the Reveille. Then, wreaths are laid by both German and British dignitaries, readings are delivered in both German and English, there are prayers for peace, and singing of both national anthems.

It is a wonderfully heartening demonstration of reconciliation; a fantastic statement of peace and hope for the future.

SHALOM, JACK

KAMMERSTEIN - CLARITY AT LAST

I had known that Jack's aircraft crashed near the village of Kammerstein for some years when, completely out of the blue, I received the following email on 18 March 2013 – amazingly, just two days after the 68th anniversary of the crash:

> "Hello Michael,
> my name is Melanie Greiner from Germany, Kammerstein, the village your father is died. Long time I search for your adress.
> The peoples of Kammerstein are often think on the Lancaster who crashed next the village.
> We want to remember to your father with a stone whose, with his name and dates, on the crash place.
> The older generation can tell you a lot about the present crash, some were in their father's salvage it.
> I would like to send you pictures of the place and other thinks about this.
> The fate of the crew has been employed many people now 68 years.
> Last week we have an article about the crash in the newspaper.
> I am so glad to be finally found you.
> Please answer me!
> Best wishes
> Melanie Greiner from Kammerstein"

I was flabbergasted but delighted to receive this. I had often wondered about the actual place of the crash, and at times thought about visiting the area to see if I could find out more about that night, and perhaps meet some people who were there at the time. Now I had been given a real opportunity and purpose for doing just that.

I exchanged lots of information, photographs etc with Melanie over the next few weeks, and it did not take me long to decide to go to Kammerstein to get as much information as I could. Melanie prepared the ground admirably for me, as will become apparent.

SHALOM, JACK

In the meanwhile, Ron drew my attention to an article by a reporter Robert Gerner in a German newspaper *Nord Bayern* (North Bavaria) dated 16 March 2013, two days before the incredible email from Melanie. A translation of key parts of the article made me realise that there were apparently eye-witnesses to the crash of Jack's aircraft, and that made my going to Kammerstein even more compelling. This is a liberal translation:

"You could put a house in the crater

Today, 68 years ago, a British bomber crashed on a field near Kammerstein, remembers witness Georg Rahnhöfer, 83. The English Lancaster bomber crashed in the last weeks of the war in a field next to the current federal highway 466 and exploded in a huge fireball. But what happened to the crew? Where was the aircraft debris taken? Many questions are still unanswered today.

Now, 68 years later, Volker Bauer has brought together three witnesses at the crash site - Leonhard Heubeck, Georg Rahnhöfer and Heinrich Volkert – and some debris, the only thing remaining of the British bomber, because there are no written documents. Literally everything went up in smoke during the last days of the war.

But at least there are still people like Georg Rahnhöfer around to bear witness. The 83-year-old from Haag was then, on 16 March 1945, 15-years-old. When the sirens howled shortly after midnight, he jumped out of bed and climbed into a makeshift shelter with several other residents of Haag. He did not have to dress. 'At the time, we went to sleep with our clothes on because there was a bomb alert almost every night,' he recalls. Rahnhöfer's father turned on the radio, and they heard reports that large Allied bomber units were travelling in a north-eastern direction towards Middle Franconia.

Two bombers shot down

Soon, there were dozens, perhaps more than a hundred, aircraft in the sky. There was an anti-aircraft gun position in the area, but it was not fired. Instead, the Wehrmacht sent up its own airplanes in the air to engage the bomber formations in aerial battles. According to Georg Rahnhöfer, two British bombers were shot down over Schwabach. One hit Schwabach near Penzendorfer Strasse, the other not far from Kammerstein near the so-called Katzenweiher, but on the other side of today's Bundesstraße 466.

Because the Lancaster which crashed next to Kammerstein, the 'Kammerstein Lancaster' still had its bomb cargo on board, it exploded with force on impact. 'We felt the pressure wave in Haag, two kilometres away,' says Georg Rahnhöfer. In nearby Kammerstein, power lines were demolished, and roofs partially blown off, tells Heinrich Volkert, then seven years old. There was a huge crater at the crash site. 'So big and so deep, you could have put a house in there,' says eye-witness Rahnhöfer.

Crew member caught

But what happened to the seven-man crew? At least one English soldier parachuted out of the plane in time, and landed unharmed in a meadow near Haag. Georg Rahnhöfer's father, one of the few in Haag who did not have to go to war because of his important position with the Schwabach company Schmauser, challenged the man with a rifle. He repeatedly called in his broken English, 'Hands up, hands up,' tells Rahnhöfer. After a short time, the Englishman surrendered and called 'Help, help'.

'There was a long consideration of what they should do with him,' recalls the 83-year-old Rahnhöfer. First, Nazis from Schwabach wanted to take him away. But then the Wehrmacht stepped in and took him, probably to a prisoner-of-war camp. But at the latest in Schwabach, his trail loses. Until his evacuation, as Georg Rahnhöfer remembers, 'the mood was by no means hostile.'

After daybreak, Rahnhöfer saw another crew member near the plane crash site - dead, his face disfigured by the explosion. In the next few days, one or two parachutes were found. Did other crew members survive and then succeed to get behind the fast approaching front? That is unclear.

Hardly any documents

Even in Kammerstein the airplane crash is not documented in writing. 'From that period in time we have very few documents,' laments Leonhard Heubeck, who for many years has looked after the municipal archive. Heubeck, born in 1935, like Rahnhöfer from Haag, remembers the crash of the bomber as a ten-year-old. He tried to get to the impact site the day after the crash in vain. 'We were curious,' says Heubeck. 'And we had little else to do because we had no schooling from the beginning of 1945.' He could only see the crash site from afar. 'SS people scared us away.'

What is left of the British Lancaster is stored in a bucket in the Volker Bauer's basement: an old alternator; parts of the Plexiglas cover, behind which the Gunner was sitting; bent iron parts; the glass of a Pilot's goggles. Whenever the field is freshly ploughed, Bauer searches for new debris. But it is rare to find anything spectacular. 'The huge hole was naturally levelled after the war with construction debris and all sorts of things,' the municipal council suspects.

Looking for photos

Bauer does not give up hope, however, that in an attic somewhere might still be an historical photo of that time, which could bring a little more light on the situation. Until that time, he's trying to question witnesses - Contemporary witnesses like Georg Rahnhöfer. The then 15-year-old had to go to war. In early April 1945 he was moved into Schwabach barracks, together with many other conscripts. They were to be the last contingent of the supposedly 1000-year-old Reich. After a few days of training in Schwabach, Rahnhöfer and his comrades were brought to Neuburg on the Danube via Roth, Thalmässing, Titting and Eichstätt. In the early morning of 19 April 1945, he escaped. Deserted. He travelled on foot and then as a passenger on a motorbike, he got himself back home, to his mother's arms, on April 20, the day after the Americans took Schwabach (and Kammerstein).

The war was over for Rahnhöfer and for the region."

The evidence of Georg Rahnhöfer was fascinating and consistent with what was known to me, or I had surmised. Thus, he had correctly identified that two Lancasters crashed in the area (RF154 and PD275); the capture of another crew member landing by parachute nearby was consistent with Ted's story; his evidence of the scale of the explosion showed the 4000 lb 'Cookie' exploded on hitting the ground; and crucially he had seen Jack at the crash scene. But it was still not clear how Jack got to be 'near the plane crash site.' And I noted that he did not find Jack until the next day – what had happened in the meanwhile?

My trip to Kammerstein now took on a greater significance.

It did not take me long to put together my plans. I would fly to Nürnberg via Amsterdam, returning by the same route. I would expect to arrive in Nürnberg at 13.45 on Tuesday 28 May. The journey by car from Nüremberg Airport is only 35 minutes, but allowing time to collect the car etc, my expected arrival time in Kammerstein would be around 14.45 or perhaps 15.00. I would drive direct to Hotel Meyerle in Kammerstein where I had made a reservation. My return flight from Nürnberg was on Friday 31 May, departing at 14.20, so I plan to leave Kammerstein at about 12.00.

Each evening of my trip, I wrote a daily report and emailed it to Ron, Leila, Lynn and Leila's older daughter, Janice. I have integrated these reports, with some light editing and re-ordering where I had added things later, as follow:

Tuesday 28 May 2013

"Well, it has been a long day! It started at 5.30am, and all went well until my 9.20am flight from Birmingham was delayed 20 mins. This should have given me sufficient time to catch my transfer flight from Amsterdam to Nürnberg, as the original schedule gave me 55mins, but what with complicated Security for flight connections and the sheer scale of Schipol Airport, I just made it by the skin of my teeth, all hot and out of breath.

Flying into Nürnberg Airport, looking out from my window seat, I thought of the irony, the poignancy, the contrast between me in a modern jet aircraft with all mod cons and in

SHALOM, JACK

total safety and broad sunny daylight, and the experience of Jack's last flight, in no more than a rattling and cold flying suitcase, with flak all around in total darkness and the worst of dangers. My view of Nürnberg was of a modern and confident city....

I picked up the car OK and thank goodness I had satnav (stick-on type), because I doubt I would have found the hotel otherwise. Let us just say it was not at all easy. The hotel seemed closed down when I arrived, but I eventually got someone from the kitchen(!) to let me in and into my room.

I had a short wait before being collected by Melanie - including husband Michael, 11-year-old daughter Mia, and 1-year-old daughter Talia. We drove to a huge wheat-field, and with the help of GPS location and walking out into the field, came to the actual site. I have some photographs, which I will send in due course, but there is naturally enough nothing to see. I am told that when the wheat has been harvested and the field ploughed, it is possible to see a depression in the field where the aircraft came to rest and exploded. The flightpath was described to me. It is a blessing that there was nothing around – the crash site is a good way from the nearest building.

75 - The crash site near Kammerstein, looking NNE towards Nürnberg, the direction from which the burning aircraft came

76 - Melanie Greiner local historian and Kammerstein resident, with daughter Talia at the crash site

This evening was spent with the family at their home having a typical local meal of boiled potatoes, local grilled sausages (thin and dark, with herbs), sauerkraut and dry rye bread - washed down in my case with some local beer.

I delivered some gifts to each of them (I forgot to mention 8-year-old Samuel and 18-year-old Fabian), which I think were well-received. Michael's grandmother lives with them, and there was a gift for her too, but she is having a spell in hospital.

Kammerstein is a small sleepy and very old village, somewhat chaotic as to layout, but peaceful and relaxed. They do not seem to bother to keep it tidy or orderly at all (and that is putting it mildly as far as Melanie's house and garden are concerned). Life is pretty basic and simple here.

The weather has been perfect, but the forecast for tomorrow is heavy rain all day. I will probably go to Schwabach to visit the cemetery where Jack was first buried immediately after the crash. I am due to meet four eye-witnesses of the crash, on-site, on Thursday, when the weather might be a bit better. That will be the most important part of the trip for me."

Wednesday 29 May 2013

"I have had a lovely day. I stayed in the hotel this morning, catching up on emails and preparing for my meeting with eye-witnesses tomorrow. I first had a big breakfast (in Continental terms) because I was actually quite hungry and knew I would not have time for lunch. I was collected at 1pm and taken to the New Cemetery, Schwabach. This is as lovely as a cemetery can be, and certainly the most beautiful and peaceful I have seen, set in woodland and carefully laid out (pardon the use of that term) as well as being tidily kept. The area where Jack was originally buried (along with the crew of another Lancaster - and others over the next few weeks before the war finally ended) was pointed out to me. It is now simply part of the cemetery and one would not know of its earlier use unless told. We also visited a small plaque in the ground commemorating a child Melanie and

Michael had, who sadly died at birth (Zoe, 2003). I could not bring myself to ask more.

77 - Entrance to Schwabach New Cemetery

78 - The path now dividing the area of the temporary communal grave where Jack and six airmen from the crashed Lancaster PD275 were originally buried

We then walked around the old district of Schwabach, a delightful area (even in the rain). We saw the Synagogue, the Talmud School (up for sale) and the Rabbi's house, as well as the usual important buildings (*Rathaus* [Town Hall] etc).

Schwabach is noted for its goldsmithing, but I managed to get a few gifts nonetheless!

I went back with Melanie and her family and spent the rest of the day with them. They really have taken me into their lives and been extraordinarily generous with their time and hospitality. We all sat round the kitchen table putting the world to right and learning more about how people of all nations are really similar. Melanie offered tea and coffee and produced a huge home-made (of course) cheesecake that would sit very comfortably in the window of the best patisseries anywhere. But what struck me even more was that it tasted so much like the ones my dear mother Sadie used to make - with home-made cream-cheese too, naturally. How poignant, given the reason why I was there. I confess that this was the first time on the trip that my emotions began to swell....

I was also so very struck by the nature of this family. The ages of the four children range from 1 to 18, but they all interact so well with each other and their parents. The three older siblings play with and are very caring of the baby. The family lives very modestly, simple home-cooked (and often home-grown) food all served from dishes at the table, drinking water mostly; casual (and I suspect not many) clothes; getting on with life and bothering no-one; always looking out for each other and their community. A truly lovely family with the best set of values imaginable. And I feel so humble at the way they have opened up their lives and allowed me to share them.

I joined them in the family evening meal of *Sauerbraten*,[107] white asparagus and *Klösse*[107] - I must look that up when I get back and give you all the recipe: it seems to be a dumpling, but is much lighter and whiter, made of potatoes, eggs, flour, and breadcrumbs. It is absolutely delicious, and the meal as cooked was honestly one of the best I have ever tasted. The sauce was out of this world.

We chatted for a long time about all kinds of things - economies, energy policy, bringing up children in today's world, prisons (I talk about them since I started my volunteering in one), Lady Godiva, the Coventry story, and of course loads on football!

Mia (aged 11) delighted me by presenting me with an illustrated postcard around the word "Thanks", drawn and coloured with the water colour pencil set I brought for her. I was very touched.

Tomorrow I am going to watch Mia play in her local football team (she is as keen on the game as the men in the whole family - Melanie's father coaches local kids too). In the afternoon we meet at the crash site with three or four eye-witnesses. I have marshalled my questions, with Melanie's father acting as interpreter and Melanie as scribe. I will go back to the house afterwards and doubtless eat there again. I will take my tablet and share with them some of the many photographs I have stored on it - but will not bore them, I have promised. I spent some time in the evening looking at Melanie's local history collection (which includes boxes of postcards about the area).

I will make my way back to the airport on Friday after breakfast - another challenge, hopefully met by the hired satnav!

Meanwhile, after a lovely day I hope to have a lovely night's sleep. It is an hour ahead of the UK here, so I hope to be fast asleep while you are still dozing in front of the TV."

Thursday 30 May 2013

"The day here has started bright with sunny intervals, although rain is forecast. Let's hope it stays dry, not only while we shout from the touchline, but also when we are standing at the side of the wheat-field crash site. Melanie's father will help with translation, while Melanie will be the scribe. Whatever the weather, it promises to be quite a day, and the last before I make my way home tomorrow (Friday) morning.

The morning was spent watching a junior football tournament (9-13-year olds). It started quite early, so I caught the last of three games. Mia's team, JFG Aurachtal, was in the tournament. She was the only girl in the team, and indeed she was one of only two girls I saw amongst the six or eight teams in the tournament. They won 2-0, very convincingly, and as Mia was playing central defence she had little to do. Unfortunately, the team lost their earlier two games..... but I was given the honour of posing with the team for the group photograph!

Samuel also came to watch. He was frustrated that he was not playing (he is 8 and the age range starts at 9). But he delighted me by wearing the Coventry City shirt I brought for him as a gift (there were small gifts for each member of the family). I told him that he had the only CCFC shirt in the whole of Germany. Considering that when I arrived he was wearing a Barcelona FC shirt, you can see how thoughtful he was (his choice, not his Mum's) and how chuffed was I.

Before the meeting with eye-witnesses, we went back to the house to finish off the delicious cheesecake, and I showed Melanie and Michael all the photographs and documents I have of my father (on my tablet), as well as many family photographs.

Please note that I have been very matter of fact about what follows. It will be somewhat distressing, but I cannot find a better way to write this down - and written it must be. My apologies in advance.

The key part of the day was, of course, meeting with the eye-witnesses. This was somewhat chaotic. First of all, only one of the witnesses could recall seeing my father or could add anything to what we know already. He was Geog Rahnhöfer, who was 15 at the time (so now aged 83). He had much to say [and had already said it all to the newspaper *Nord Bayern*] about his experiences at the time and also about one of the crew who he said he saw baling out. In a nutshell (and missing out the times he gave, which are certainly wrong), he said he heard the 'plane coming down and went out of the bunker (air-raid shelter) he was in to see it coming from the direction of Nürnberg; it was on fire and unstable. He did not see it actually crash as he was then a few km away in Haag. But he began to walk to where the 'plane was headed, sheltering from danger on the way. He heard a loud explosion as the 'plane crashed (it was said to have been heard 5km away). On the way, he saw bits of wreckage which he said he saw falling from the 'plane as it was coming down. He particularly referred to seeing wreckage in Schattenhof. When he got there, the 'plane was still on fire but the flames were dying down. He said he saw my father about 10m from the crater, lying on his back. There was a lot of blood on his face but not elsewhere on his body. He said the face was disfigured and he could not discern a nose. The next reliable thing to record is that the next morning, two young women (members of some kind of Home Guard, as I interpreted) came with two ponies pulling a cart and put my father's body in a wooden box - believing it already contained other bodies they had collected. He

SHALOM, JACK

understood they took the bodies to Schwabach. There are couple of things to say about this testimony. Firstly, to restate he was 15-years-old, and that this was 68 years ago. But the times he gave are not consistent with other information. He thought the crash occurred at about 1am and that he arrived at the site between 6.30 and 7am. The 1am guess is miles out - as shown from the time reported by the German Luftwaffe (and from the testimony of surviving crew as assembled by Ron). Secondly, it is not clear why it would have taken him until 6.30 or 7.00am to get there from a few kilometres away in Haag. Others present thought the crash was earlier (correctly). One must remember these were all frightened children, probably without watches. But apart from timings I have no reason to doubt the essence of his testimony. There was some discussion about how the body managed to get out of the crashed 'plane. From what we know, I have no doubt that it was thrown there from the explosion - any suggestion that my father was alive when the 'plane crashed and managed to get out after the crash and explosion of the 4000lb bomb is, in my view fantasy.

Other witnesses could add little but did not doubt Georg's account.

79 - With eye-witnesses to the crash and items found at the crash site. From left to right: Georg Rahnhöfer, Hermine Schilling, Leonhard Heubeck, and me, 30 May 2013

SHALOM, JACK

The chaos was due to a lot of cross-talk and a couple of interferences. In particular, a local politician, Volker Bauer, was claiming credit for 'finding' me and uncovering a lot of the story. He has been to Dürnbach and Gmund and has assembled his own file. He is standing for election next September and is seeking publicity and kudos from all this. He had a member of the press from Schwabach there, complete with video camera, despite my express wishes for this to be low key and personal. We dealt with that, but nonetheless it added to the chaos, with several conversations and interjections. He is the person wanting to erect a commemorative stone near the site, and although I am relaxed about that I am advised that this is for his benefit, not for any altruistic reason. The fact that he already is trying to set a date in July (ie before the elections) rather than wait until next year is perhaps evidence of his intent.

Anyway, that aside, I believe we have that further piece of the jigsaw puzzle. Melanie is going to get a better fix on the time the two women came with the cart, and another check on times from a witness who was not there today.

But even after about 1½ hours with witnesses I still have a couple of questions. Regardless of the actual times, it must have been several hours between the crash and the two women coming to collect the body. Was it just left there as everyone went about their business? How could the other eye-witnesses not have seen it? Melanie will try to clarify - one living witness was not present yesterday (Volker Bauer's uncle).

Volker Bauer had brought with him a box of small items said to be pieces of wreckage, which have come to the surface when the field has been ploughed. They were mangled bits of metal, Perspex(?) fragments a few centimetres across, an electric motor and some more personal items - a spoon and the lens from spectacles come to mind. He asked if I wanted any of it. I declined, saying it was like picking over the dead. He did not like that, but that's how I felt.

Georg Rahnhöfer had a story about him being a deserter, but the dates did not add up. He was certainly in the Hitler Youth (he had no choice) but his story that he had deserted before the crash and was in hiding in his home village (Haag) does not make sense for his age. The newspaper report Melanie sent me a few weeks ago says he deserted later, but he would have had to have been called up into the army in the last weeks of the war - the Americans took the area on 19 April 1945.

After the meeting we went for a walk in the woods around Kammerstein. I had mentioned in passing my walks in Sutton Park and recent holiday walking in North Devon, so they built in this treat just for me. It was only when we were about halfway through the planned walk that they mentioned the *Zechen* (singular *Zeche*), which are tiny insects (I guess they are so classified - they are too small to see any legs let alone count them!). These get in everywhere and suck blood, leading to possible fever and brain problems! I began to itch just thinking about them...but so far, so good - I think!

After the walk, I joined them for another family meal - a pork casserole (but as there was crackling, maybe roast first?) with home-made (of course) pasta (well, that's the nearest I can think of - it was fluffier and lighter than normal pasta), and red cabbage with small pieces of apple. It was absolutely delicious. I told Melanie that I thought she was trying to get me to stay....

Anyway, my fingers are tired from using my BlackBerry for this long report, so I will close now. The next update will be sometime after I get back home."

Friday 31 May 2013

"Well, I wanted to send another round-robin to add a few details about my trip, more for my own record than anything. But the day began just a bit badly, although all sorted now.

The weather was grim - very overcast and raining steadily (it's quite a bit better now, just drizzle) - not good for a drive on German *Autobahnen* [motorways] back to the airport. But I had plenty of time for a good Continental breakfast and careful packing, all done with time to spare to set the satnav and wind up the volume. So a last minute check on flight times..... er....can't find e-ticket or any other papers. Search. No joy. Search again. Nix. Hmm. Begin to panic, then think of strategy. Get to airport as soon as possible (I thought I might go into Schwabach for some shopping and photography, but I would better forego that). Wait. Maybe papers are in the car - not been used since arriving at the hotel as I have been fetched and carried everywhere. Go out to car in rain. No joy. Ah well. Think again. I had plastic files on the passenger seat on the journey, and they fell on the floor when I braked...under the passenger seat? Yeeeah!

Next to set the satnav. Battery flat! Has to be plugged into usual power point (used to be called the lighter socket). OK. Not OK - lead won't reach from the sensible place to put the device on the windscreen..... Get the curly cable and give it an almighty stretch. Well, reaches of a fashion. Problem solved, as long as I don't knock the cable when driving, even with it crossing the steering wheel....

I thought that before making for the airport I would drive into Kammerstein and take some pictures. When Melanie and Michael first walked me round I had left both my camera and 'phone in the car. My plan was to say my goodbyes last evening. But they wanted to come to the hotel to see me off. I could not resist strongly, as they would have been offended, so I quickly gave in, and they gave me a lovely send-off – with Mia and Talia too. I will ask Melanie to email me some pics next week.

My journey to the airport was not without incident. Apart from the horrible rain it took me a while to realise the satnav voice "Exit ahead" was advance advice (ie "There is an exit ahead") not immediate instruction "Make an exit") - so I left the motorway when I shouldn't have done so. And I did get my left and right mixed up as I did when last going to Dürnbach (Ron, Lynn and Leila might recall), due to the disorientation of driving on the right. But as far as I know I only went through one red traffic light....

So I am now in Nürnberg Airport, all relaxed and ready for home. Thank you all for reading this far (the longest email I have ever sent - assuming it does not exceed allowable size....) and for all your wishes on the way."

So, taking all the evidence so far, I drew the following conclusions:

- Jack did not get out of the aircraft before it crashed.
- All the eye-witnesses to the aircraft coming down testified that it was the normal orientation – clearly the pilot Bud Churchward had done a sterling job in keeping the Lancaster on an even keel to the extent that it crash-landed the 'right' way up.
- The 4000lb 'Cookie' exploded when the aircraft hit the ground, causing a huge crater.
- As Jack's body was said to having been found 10m from the wreckage, a plausible explanation is that it was thrown there by the force of the explosion, the canopy of his gun turret also being blown away.

However, there were still some nagging concerns:

- Georg Rahnhöfer did not see Jack's body until he reached the crash site the following morning. Although some of his timings are clearly wrong, he was consistent on this point in saying 'daybreak' in the newspaper article and 6.30 – 7.00am when I spoke with him. How could the other eye-witnesses not have seen Jack's body?
- Is it realistic for Jack to have been thrown out of the turret by the explosion but not dismembered in any way? The body was intact, albeit in his flying suit, with blood only on his disfigured face.

- According to a map constructed by Volker Bauer and sent to me by Melanie on 4 April 2013, Jack's body was found 50m from the crash site centre (map co-ordinates 49° 29' 690" North, 10° 96' 495" East), yet Georg Rahnhöfer gave the location 10m from the burning aircraft, a significant difference. Either could be true if the body had been thrown there by the force of the explosion, but it is not clear from where Volker Bauer got his information. Georg Rahnhöfer did actually see the body – Volker Bauer was not even born at the time.

- Regardless of the actual times, it must have been several hours between the crash and the two women coming to collect the body. Was it just left there as everyone went about their business?

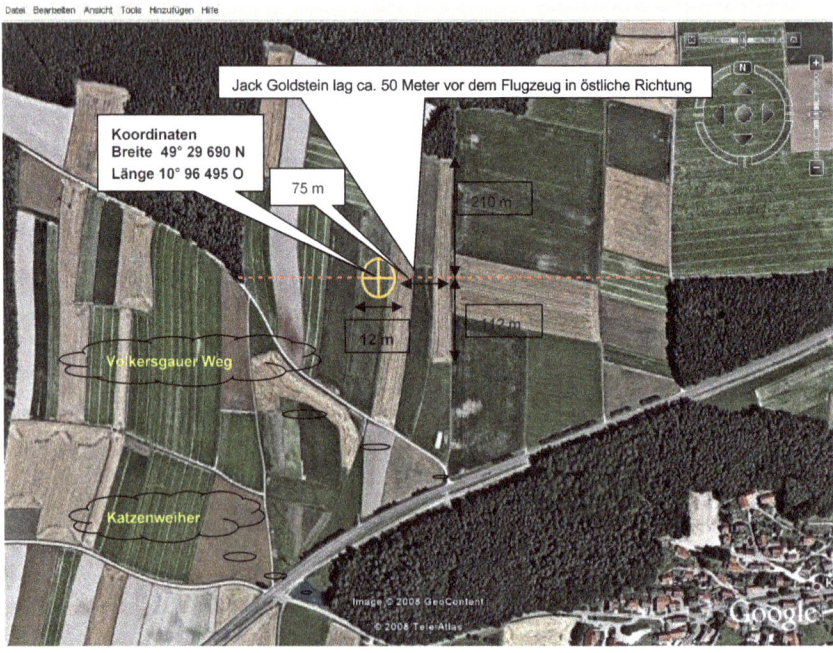

80 - Aerial photograph of the crash site with location and place where Jack's body was said to have been found. It was later realised that this was where Jack had been laid after being taken from the burning wreckage

I had further correspondence with Melanie on these points, and she spoke further with Georg Rahnhöfer. He described the crashed aircraft as 'very broken' and in his opinion no-one could climb out, so Jack must have been thrown by the explosion to where Georg found him. Melanie was able to surmise that Jack's body lay where it fell all through the night. The area was cordoned off by the SS so that no-one could get near until the two women came to take away the body later that morning. The local archivist believed the women were sent by the SS.

And then, on 1 June 2013, I received the following astonishing email from Melanie, in her broken English:

> Dear Michael,
> I'm sorry, I'm such a fool!
> In the morning it occurred to me that my grandfather, my mother's father lived near the crash site, directly behind the trees.
> I was just about to ask him if he has around him and noticed that he remembers exactly!
> Here is the statement of the witnesses Hans Muschweck,[108] 12 years old in year 1945, taken on 1 June 2013:
>> "It was late evening when we heard about 22 clock to serve, still not quite late. I ran with some other Kammersteiner to the crash site. A man sat still in the *lucke* [hatch], he did not move. Some Kammerstein people gathered to see him out of the hatch if he is still alive. They brought him a piece away from the crash spot, but presented only his death proof. We all went back to the bunker [shelter] to seek protection against further attacks.
>> Do not remember who took the man everything from the plane, but they are all already dead.
>>
>> Remember from
>> Hans Muschweck,
>> Birkenhang 1
>> 91126 Kammerstein
>> today, 14 o Clock"

At my request, Melanie questioned her grandfather Hans further, and clarified all that I needed.

SHALOM, JACK

That was it! Everything fell into place. I finally had the missing pieces of the jigsaw puzzle.

This is, then, the summary of what happened to Jack on that last flight of Lancaster RF154 AS-B on 16 March 1945, after it was hit by a German fighter aircraft at 9.31pm:

It is highly likely that Jack was already dead when the aircraft crashed, fatally shot by the JU88 that had attacked RF154 AS-B. The crash, into a field just off what is now Federal Highway 466, near the village of Kammerstein in Bavaria, caused the 4000lb 'Cookie' which was still in the bomb bay to explode. It blew off the mid-upper gun turret canopy. It left a huge crater, and the sound of the explosion was heard 5km away. There were eye-witnesses to the plane coming down, and several people ran to the crash site, including 15-year-old Georg Rahnhöfer from Haag. Amongst the people from Kammerstein who reached the crash site first was 12-year-old Hans Muschweck. When they got to the 'plane soon after it crashed, the canopy had blown off with the explosion, but Jack was still in the gun turret, his face badly injured by the blast. As Hans was just 12-years-old at the time, he watched from a distance of about 20m from where Jack was. The Kammerstein residents found Jack was already dead. They pulled him out and lay him on his back on the ground a short distance from the wrecked 'plane. At that point, Jack did not have on his flying helmet. He was not dismembered, but his face was badly disfigured. As there were more air-raids, the people of Kammerstein all rushed back to their shelters and left Jack's body where they had put it. Georg Rahnhöfer saw the body there in the following early morning. There was no-one else there, so he thought he was first on the scene. The area was cordoned off by the SS until the body was placed on a box and taken away in a horse-drawn cart by two women. They took his body to Schwabach New Cemetery, where he was buried with six other airmen from Lancaster PD275, which had crashed nearby on Penzendorfer Strasse, Schwabach. They were all reburied at the CWGC cemetery in Dürnbach on 18 June 1948.

All is clear. My mind is at ease.

SHALOM, JACK

REMEMBERING JACK

Publication of the description of Jack's last flight by Ron Goldstein on the ww2talk.com website,[7] and my own account[8] posted to the BBC WW2 project 'The People's War,' has resulted in the story being re-told in many well-regarded places.[2 3 4 5 6 11 66 109 110] Ron and I have encouraged this, so as to spread knowledge of Jack's final hours; to gain lasting recognition for his service to and sacrifice for his adopted country; to demonstrate the courage and fortitude of those in Bomber Command; and, above all, so that he may be remembered as one who gave his life in the fight for peace and freedom.

In November 1949 there was a service of dedication in the Cathedral Church of the Blessed Virgin Mary of Lincoln (Lincoln Cathedral), when Memorial Books of Numbers 1 and 5 Bomber Groups were deposited in the Airmen's Chapel of St Michael. [Jack's Squadron, 166, was in Group 1].

Jack is also mentioned in the Roll of Honour of 166 Squadron,[101] the record of Jewish service-people who died in WW2,[56] the definitive record of Bomber Command aircraft and crew losses,[111] and the Bomber Command Roll of Honour.[112]

The International Bomber Command Centre (IBCC)[113] has been created to provide a world-class facility to serve as a point for recognition, remembrance and reconciliation for Bomber Command. It was formally opened on 12 April 2018. At the heart of the IBCC is the Memorial Spire, which commands stunning views across Lincoln, with a focus on the City's ancient Cathedral, which served as a sighting point for crews flying from and returning to Lincolnshire. For many of the men named on the accompanying walls, the Cathedral provided their last sight of Britain. The IBCC Memorial Spire is now recognised as the UK's tallest war memorial. It was awarded the 2016 Structural Steel Design Award and was officially unveiled October 2015. Made from Corten weathering steel, it is 102ft (31.09m) high, the wingspan of the Avro Lancaster bomber, and 16ft (5m) wide at the base, the width

SHALOM, JACK

of a Lancaster wing. Surrounding the spire are the 23 Walls of Names in a series of circles framing the view of the City and the Cathedral. The Walls remember 57,871 men and women who lost their lives serving or supporting Bomber Command during WW2. There are 270 individual panels. Each one is formed from engraved sheets of Corten Weathering Steel. Every life lost in Bomber Command was equal in sacrifice, and as a result the walls do not recognise rank or medals awarded. Jack's name is obviously recorded on the walls (panel number 40); and personal, service and last operation information is in the IBCC Losses Database.

The National Memorial Arboretum (NMA) at Alrewas,[114] just a few miles from where I now live in Lichfield, is one of my favourite places on Earth. It is "the UK's year-round centre of Remembrance; a spiritually uplifting place which honours the fallen, recognises service and sacrifice, and fosters pride in our country. It is a living and lasting memorial…. It's not a cemetery. It's a place of life, represented by the 30,000 trees planted here, where older and younger generations alike can wander and wonder. Covering 150 acres, the Arboretum has something for everyone. For some it's a wonderful place to stroll and enjoy the trees; for others it's a peaceful and beautiful place to remember loved ones, particularly those who made the ultimate sacrifice for their country. The trees and the more than 300 dedicated memorials on [the] site make the Arboretum a living tribute that will forever acknowledge the personal sacrifices made by the Armed Forces and civil services of this country."[114]. The NMA has a special place in Jack's story, not only because of what it is, but also because Jack is personally commemorated there by:

- A stone paviour in the circle of paving around the stunning memorial at the focus of the Royal Air Forces Association Remembrance Garden, inscribed with his name, Jacob (Jack) Goldstein, and the RAF 'wings' emblem.

- A wooden bench (number 547) overlooking the Royal Air Forces Association memorial, bearing a plaque:

> *In loving and eternal memory of*
> *Sergeant Jacob (Jack) Goldstein,*

SHALOM, JACK

RAFVR 166 Squadron, who gave his life on 16 March 1945 to save mankind from tyranny.
SHALOM

- An oak tree in the Armed Services Wood (area 66, tree 276), marked with a plaque bearing the *Magen Dovid*[97] and the inscription:

In memory of
Sergeant Jacob (Jack) Goldstein
RAFVR 166 Squadron
Killed in action over
Nürnberg
16th March 1945

Of course, this book will provide a unique, lasting tribute to Jack, something tangible by which he is remembered. I hope so.

81 - Bench in memory of Jack at the National Memorial Arboretum (NMA), adjacent to the RAF Association Memorial

82 - Plaque attached to the bench

83 – Jack's paviour at the NMA around the RAF Association Memorial

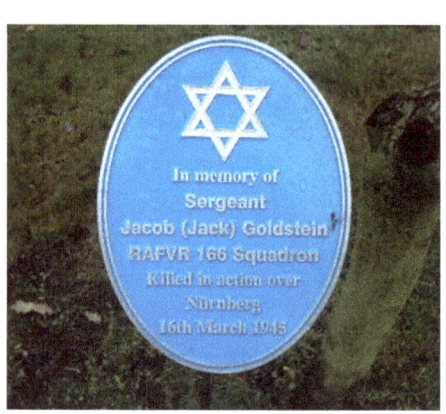

85 - Plaque designating Jack's memorial oak tree at the NMA

84 – Jack's oak tree at the NMA

SHALOM, JACK

REFLECTIONS

When I began to write this book, I thought it would be a simple matter of bringing together all that had been written and discovered before, and that I had little new to learn or experience. How naive I was. This project has been a good example of how the whole can be so much more than the constituent parts. Bringing together the stories of Jack's origins in Poland; how he and his parents came to the UK; his formative years in London's East End – the deprivation and struggles, more than compensated by the happiness and fulfilment of family belonging; the challenges of early married life; his induction into the RAF and his operational experiences, leading to the trauma and horror of that last flight; and finally his eternal fate and memory – these have brought me closer to Jack than I ever could have been. At times, I have struggled to hold back my emotions, even tears, but overall it has been a most fulfilling and rewarding experience. I do so hope it is for others too.

It is time to reflect further.

I am not a pacifist, but when I take in what I have read and heard about the hardship, heartbreak and appalling pain brought about by WW2 – from my own family as well as from others tied up in Jack's short life, I am bound to question the sanity of it all. And yet, here was such a compelling cause: to prevent tyranny spreading throughout Europe, let alone beyond; the extermination, literally, of the Jewish race and others deemed to be 'impure' or undesirable in a demented vision of the world; the willingness of hundreds of thousands of ordinary people to respond to the call to arms to save their values, their freedoms – the huge sacrifices, including laying down their lives for their beliefs and their country – this speaks volumes for the sanity of the response.

And what I see as so remarkable is how Jack and his immigrant family so readily and courageously fought for their adopted country – Jack the 'alien' who was turned off the Sandringham Estate because he presented a security risk; who was refused enlistment into the RAF until the country was desperately in need of more volunteers – he made the ultimate sacrifice.

SHALOM, JACK

I marvel too at the courage of those thousands of volunteers who made up Bomber Command. I have read several of the harrowing stories written by aircrew, not only by the survivors of Jack's last flight. The courage and fortitude shown by these volunteers – often so very young - carrying out horrendously dangerous air-raids, in the crudest of conditions, has taken away my breath. To say they have my admiration is so much of an understatement. The statistics of Bomber Command are frightening: between 3 September 1939 and 7/8 May 1945, out of 387,416 sorties, 8,953 aircraft were lost (plus 1,368 operational crashes in the UK while outward or inward bound on operational flights).[62] In the period to 31 May 1947, out of about 125,000 aircrew who served in squadrons and the operational training and conversion units, 55,500 aircrew lost their lives (so there was a 44% chance of being killed); 9,838 crew were taken as prisoners of war, many of whom were wounded; 8,403 other crew were wounded. An astonishing figure of nearly 60% of aircrew became casualties.[62] From 166 Squadron alone, there were 175 Bombers destroyed,[62] and 1048 men lost their lives.[101]

I have also been immeasurably impressed and humbled by the contribution of Canadians to Bomber Command, with 9,919 losing their lives.[61]

I know some of their later raids of Bomber Command were controversial, knowingly causing untold misery and carnage amongst the civilian populations, but I have come to accept the necessity. I grew up in wartime London and experienced the terror of the Blitz and the rocket attacks; I worked in Coventry right opposite the ruins of the Cathedral for 21 years and understood the misery and human tragedy of the German destruction of that great City. Yes, such acts in which Jack was involved are abhorrent, but there have been times when they were justified.

I recall how amazing it was to visit Kammerstein and feel the friendliness and hospitality of some of its residents – including several who had suffered greatly in the war. They were only too pleased to help me unravel the events of 16 March 1945, the night when a mass of bombers, Jack's being one of them, came to cause unimaginable damage and destruction of their area, certainly killing hundreds of their fellow-countrymen and even their relatives and friends. Their forgiveness and tolerance were truly humbling and unforgettable.

Finding out what really did happen to Jack on his last RAF flight has been enormously important to me. Long gone are the hopes and dreams that he survived and that he would suddenly appear in my life. Long gone too are the rumours – that he was shot and killed while baling out, or that he was captured and murdered by the SS. Now I know, beyond all doubt, as much as I need to know, my mind is at ease, my grief and sadness sensibly directed.

I know it is common for those who lose a parent when they are children to put that parent on a pedestal. I have tried to resist this. But I confess to having unbending love, respect and admiration for Jack, the father I did not really know, for him as an airman, my hero, but also for Jack the husband, sibling and son. I do feel I know him better than I would have done had he not been killed, albeit in a different way, and that writing this book has given me that confidence and closeness I am seeking to portray.

Had my father survived the war, I would almost certainly have been brought up to be more religious than I am now. I am not a practising Jew, but I am immensely proud of my Jewish background. For whatever reason, I feel it has shaped my life and values, and continues to do so. Both strands of my family, just one or two generations before me, the Goldsteins and the Goldbergs, arrived in England with virtually no physical assets, no English, and no cultural immersion or preparation. But they came wanting to be part of this country, and with a passionate desire for their children to be free from hate, intolerance and even persecution. They brought energy, a powerful work ethic, a strong sense of personal and community responsibility, and a commitment to citizenship and the common good. Their capacity for enjoying life with a sense of values, of hope, enterprise, and ambition has trickled down through the generations. My grandparents, on both Sadie's and Jack's sides, would have every reason to be immensely proud of their descendants. The current obsession with the negative aspects of immigration needs to be seen in this context.

I sometimes ponder how my life would have been different had Jack been one of those who returned from the war; and also what life he would have had. More often than that, I wonder what he would have made of my life as it has turned out, and sometimes this has been a great motivator; after all, we all wish our parents to be proud of us, don't we?

I end this section, Reflections, and the substance of this book, with two quotes, both from Sadie.

86 - Sadie in her 80s

The first is the final paragraph she wrote in her memoirs of her life with Jack, written in November 1987:[10]

> "Today, having lost also my second husband, my dear Alf, God rest his soul, I am comforted by the knowledge that my children and grandchildren love me as dearly as I love them."

What more could any of us ask?

And finally, the single word Sadie wrote in the book of remembrance at Dürnbach War Graves Cemetery in July 1979, next to Jack's name:

> *"Shalom!"*

Shalom, Jack.

SHALOM, JACK

CHRONOLOGY

Goldstein heritage   Goldberg heritage   Jack and Sadie

1835	Meir Goldsztejn [Goldstein] born
1845	Malke Blumsztejn [Bloomstein] born
1850s	Meir and Malke, married and living in Radzymin, near Warsaw
1878-85[115]	Gedaliah Yosef [Joe] Goldberg born in Końskowola, Poland
1883	Yosef [Joseph] Goldstein born (probably in Radzymin)
1884	Feigele [Fanny] Kamen born (probably in Warsaw)
1885-88[115]	Leah Kaufman born
1902	Yosef Goldstein and Feigele Kamen marry in Poland (probably in Warsaw)
1907	Joe Goldberg arrives in London from Końskowola, Poland
1911	16 January: Joe Goldberg and Leah Kaufman marry in London
1912	7 April: Jacob [Jack] Goldstein born in Poland to Feigele and Yosef
1913	17 September: Sarah [Sadie] Goldberg born in London to Joe and Leah
1913	Yosef Goldstein arrived in London
1913	November: Feigele made her journey from Poland to London, bringing Annie (aged 5), Levy [Lou] (aged 4), and Jacob [Jack] (aged 17 months)
1913	20 November: First British child to Feigele and Yosef, Esther, born

SHALOM, JACK

1914	28 July: First World War (WW1) started
1918	11 November: WW1 ended
1920	Meir Goldsztejn [Goldstein] died in Warsaw
1929	7 September: Leah Goldberg (née Kaufman) died
1934	25 January: Jack Goldstein and Sadie Goldberg marry in London
1934	25 April: Leila born to Sadie and Jack
1935	15 December: Malke Goldsztejn (née Blumsztejn) died in London
1939	1 May: Michael born to Sadie and Jack
1939	1 September: Second World War (WW2) started
1944	22 January: Jack enlisted into RAF Volunteer Reserve
1945	5 January: Jack posted to 166 Squadron at Kirmington, Lincolnshire
1945	16 March: Jack killed in action over Nürnberg, Germany; crashes on outskirts of Kammerstein
1945	17 March: Jack's body taken from Kammerstein and buried in Schwabach New Cemetery in a common grave, Allied Plot Grave No 1, with six airmen from Lancaster PD275
1945	8 May: WW2 ended in Europe (but continued in the Far East until 15 August 1945)
1948	18 June: Jack reburied at CWGC War Graves Cemetery, Dürnbach, Bavaria, Plot XI, Row K, Grave No 22
1950	22 August: Gedaliah Yosef [Joe] Goldberg died
1958	30 August: Yosef [Joseph] Goldstein died in London
1977	15 October: Feigele [Fanny] Goldstein (née Kamen) died in London

SHALOM, JACK

1979	30 July (?): Sadie's first and only visit to Dürnbach War Graves Cemetery
2001	7 January: Sarah [Sadie] Goldstein (née Goldberg) died in London
2012	25 April: Ron and Nita Goldstein, with Leila and her younger daughter Lynn, and I visited Dürnbach War Graves Cemetery
2013	18 March: Surprise first email from Melanie Greiner (née Herzog), local historian from Kammerstein
2013	29 May: My first visit to Schwabach New Cemetery
2013	30 May: My first visit to the crash site on the outskirts of Kammerstein, meeting three eye-witnesses to the crash
2013	1 June: Hans Muschweck (Melanie Greiner's maternal grandfather) made his eye-witness statement that finally settles the question of Jack's fate

SHALOM, JACK

LIST OF PHOTOGRAPHS AND ILLUSTRATIONS

1. Meir Goldstein and his wife Malke (with granddaughter Fay, daughter of Yancze and Choomah) – p10

2. Feigele and Yosef in 1914 with children (left to right) Jack, Esther, Annie, and Lou – p13

3. Houses in Boreham Street, Bethnal Green, London – p16

4. Ron Goldstein's sketch of the layout of 21 Boreham Street – p20

5. From left to right: Ronnie, Debby, Mick, and Polly – p26

6. With friends: Polly far left; Mick with cap; Ron front row left; Debby far right – p26

7. Polly in swim-suit – p27

8. Annie – p33

9. Esther – p33

10. Gertie – p33

11. Jack – p34

12. Jean – p34

13. Personal information statement of Gedaliah (Joe) Goldberg – p37

14. Sadie and Ben as children with their mother Leah and grandmother – p40

15. Four Goldberg children. From left to right: Ralph (8), Sid (6), Morry (4), and Freda (2) – p40

16. Joe Goldberg in khaki drill uniform worn by soldiers in the tropics in WW1 – p41

17. London Rifles 'C' Company March 1918. Joe Goldberg is in the third row from the bottom, 5th from the left – p41

18. Joe Goldberg's army souvenirs: message pouch, medals, sew-on Regiment badge, and badge (or epaulette) for his Small Box Respirator (gas mask) – p41

19. Joe Goldberg, taken on a march in Hyde Park, London. The reverse says: 'To my loving children J S and L Goldstein' (Jack, Sadie and Leila) but not mentioning me, so must be dated after Leila's birth year but before mine, ie between 1934 and 1939 – p41

20. Sadie, Jack, sister Leila and me, probably 1943, before Jack enlisted – p44

21. With Leila outside 60 Fairholt Road, about 1946 – p46

22. Goldberg siblings from left to right: Sid, Freda, and Morry – p49

23. Brothers Ben (left) and Morry (right) – p49

24. Ralph – p49

25. Sid – p49

26. Yosef Goldstein as a fire guard in WW2 – p50

27. Yosef Goldstein's workshop in Great Eastern Street. Yosef is back centre wearing an apron, in front of a model; to his left in spectacles is Mr Tan, his partner; Jack is on the left at a bench, wearing a tie; Lou is on the right between two women, towards the back at a machine, with Ronnie opposite – p52

28. Mossy – p54
29. Debby – p54
30. Polly – p54
31. Mick – p55
32. Ronnie – p55
33. Lou – p55
34. Sadie and Jack, probably late 1944 or early 1945. The last family photograph before he was killed – p56
35. Blackpool County Borough correspondence of July 1944 regarding reception and processing by the town of 800 mothers and children evacuees. Reproduced with kind permission of the Heritage Service, Blackpool Council – p58
36. From left to right: Jacob Szmidek ('Smith') and his second wife, Ruchze (Rene); Herschel and his daughter Esther; Yosef and Feigele; Yancze and his wife Choomah – p61
37. Feigele and Yosef, before WW2 – p61
38. Feigele and Yosef, mid-1950s – p61
39. Feigele, shortly after breaking her arm, aged 90 – p61
40. Lou Goldstein's Alien Registration Certificate, showing an updated photograph, his change of name to Grayson, and his army service dates – p65
41. Jack, shortly after enlisting on 22 January 1944. The white 'flash' insert in his side cap indicates that he was still in training – p66

SHALOM, JACK

42. Service Record (side 1), showing personal details including Polish nationality, his sleight build, and religion as 'Hebrew' – p66

43. Service Record (side 2), showing the posting restriction due to being Polish, and the recording of his being killed in action – p66

44. Service Record (side 3), showing Regrading and promotion to Sergeant – p67

45. Service Record (side 4), detailing postings – p67

46. The crew of RF154, taken in 1945. From left to right - Front row: ground crew, Jack Goldstein, Bud Churchward Back row: Chuck Goddard, ground crew, Alf White, Lefty Etherington, ground crew, Ted Hull, Bob Green - p68

47. Flight Crew and ground crew, with Jack in the centre, 1945 – p71

48. Jack with Bob Green by the rear gun turret – p77

49. Alf White in the astrodome – p77

50. Jack in full flying gear – p77

51. Taken from the astrodome. Jack in his mid-upper gun turret on the way to a daylight operation over Essen, 11 March 1945, just five days before he was killed – p77

52. From left to right: Ted Hull, Jack, and Bob Green – p79

53. From left to right: Bud Churchward, Bob Green, Jack, and Ted Hull – p79

54. 166 Squadron Order of Battle No. 232, 16 March 1945 – p80

55. Aerial view of crash crater, taken by Allies, 9 April 1945 – p86

56. German fighter claims 16-17 March 1945 – p87

57. Crash locations 16-17 March 1945 – p88

58. Official report of the fate of the crew of RF154 – p97

59. Report of exhumation of Jack's body, 24 June 1947 – p98

60. Graves Concentration Report for reburial at Dürnbach of Jack and the six airmen of Lancaster PD275 killed the same night and originally buried with him in Schwabach New Cemetery – p99

61. Jack's medals. From left to right, they are: The 1939-1945 Star with Bomber Command Clasp; The France and Germany Star; The War Medal 1939-1945 – p103

62. Photographs taken by a local resident of the site of the crash of PD275 from 12 Squadron in which six of the seven-man crew were killed, as were nine civilians on the ground at Schwabach, 16 March 1945 – p113

63. Jack's temporary grave marker at Dürnbach War Graves Cemetery – p117

64. Entrance Lodge at Dürnbach, containing the Register and Book of Remembrance – p124

65. Pergola and rest-shelter at Dürnbach – p124

66. Jack's gravestone is in the centre of view – p124

67. Jack's gravestone. Dedication is:
    FOR EVER REMEMBERED
      WIFE SADIE CHILDREN
        LEILA AND MICHAEL
       PARENTS AND FAMILY – p124

68. 'Their Name Liveth For Evermore' is a promise fulfilled – p124

69. Group visit to Dürnbach 2012. From left to right: Leila, Lynn, me, Ron, and Nita – p127

70. Ron in discussion with Paul Willing, Head Gardener at Dürnbach War Graves Cemetery – p127

71. Dignitaries, servicemen and women, and members of the public join in the Remembrance Day Ceremony at Dürnbach War Graves Cemetery – p130

72. Servicemen from several nations join in the Dürnbach Ceremony – p130

73. Wreaths from several nations around the central cross – p130

74. The final tribute – p130

75. The crash site near Kammerstein, looking NNE towards Nürnberg, the direction from which the burning aircraft came – p137

76. Melanie Greiner local historian and Kammerstein resident, with daughter Talia at the crash site – p137

77. Entrance to Schwabach New Cemetery – p139

78. The path now dividing the area of the temporary communal grave where Jack and six airmen from the crashed Lancaster PD275 were originally buried – p139

79. With eye-witnesses to the crash and items found at the crash site. From left to right: Georg Rahnhöfer, Hermine Schilling, Leonhard Heubeck, and me, 30 May 2013 – p143

80. Aerial photograph of the crash site with location and place where Jack's body was said to have been found. It was later realised that this was where Jack had been laid after being taken from the burning wreckage – p148

81. Bench in memory of Jack at the National Memorial Arboretum (NMA), adjacent to the RAF Association Memorial – p154

82. Plaque attached to the bench – p154

83. Jack's paviour at the NMA around the RAF Association Memorial – p154

84. Jack's oak tree at the NMA – p154

85. Plaque designating Jack's memorial oak tree at the NMA – p154

86. Sadie in her 80s - p158

SHALOM, JACK

REFERENCES AND NOTES

[1] I have preferred the German spelling rather than the common English 'Nuremberg' except where the latter is what is in quoted documents. I have generally used vernacular spellings of the places themselves (such as Dürnbach and Tölz) rather than Anglicised versions except in the case of Munich since the German 'München' would be far less familiar to English readers.

[2] The Aircrew Remembrance Society is a significant source of information on WW2 air crew losses. See https://www.webarchive.org.uk/wayback/archive/20121121082122/http://www.aircrewremembrancesociety.com/raf1945/3/churchyardbud.html. [Accessed 8 January 2018].

[3] See www.aircrewremembered.com/churchyard-bud.html. [Accessed 8 January 2018].

[4] 'Victory in Europe, D-Day to the fall of Berlin' by Karen Farrington, Arcturus Publishing, 2005; ISBN-13 978-0572031015.

[5] 'Reflections of War: Armageddon (27th September 1944 – May 1945) (Bomber Command)' by Martin Bowman, Pen and Sword Aviation, 2013; ASIN B00LOUT07Y.

[6] The website 'World War 2 Today' describes many WW2 incidents. See http://ww2today.com/16-march-1945-shot-down-the-fate-of-one-mid-upper-gunner. [Accessed 8 January 2018].

[7] 'The Last Flight of Lancaster RF154 (AS-B)' by Ron Goldstein at www.ww2talk.com/index.php?threads/the-last-flight-of-lancaster-rf154-as-b.36770. [Accessed 8 January 2018].

[8] I have written eight stories for the BBC WW2 People's War website, several of which are referenced in later pages, all under the pseudonym mg1939. The most pertinent in the present context is: 'The Night my Father was Killed in Action' at

http://www.bbc.co.uk/history/ww2peopleswar/stories/90/a8452190.shtml. [Accessed 9 January 2018].

[9] See http://www.facebook.com/pages/Meir-and-Malkah-Goldstein/138395832903055. [Accessed 9 January 2018]. Note that the spelling 'Malkah' is used in the Facebook title page, but the preferred spelling of 'Malke' is used in this book

[10] "And Then There Were Eleven," is a collection of memories of all the then surviving Goldstein siblings about their early lives, compiled and edited by Esther Rosenquit (née Goldstein), published privately, 1988. In 1990 it was formatted for the Jewish Care's Tapes for the Blind and became one of its listed popular Talking Books. It was then lodged in the Bishopsgate Reference Library and the Steinberg Centre, thus making it accessible to researchers. It was also used in 1993-4 by the Museum of London for its 'Peopling of London Exhibition' at the Barbican; and in 1996 by the Commission for Social Equality for its 'Roots of the Future Exhibition.'

[11] 'Three lives in Education: Reflections of an Anglo-Jewish Family' by Susy Stone, Jean Lawrence and Michael Goldstein, Clio Publishing, revised first edition 2011; ISBN 978-0-9556983-1-6.

[12] I also felt it helpful to avoid possible confusion between my two grandfathers – Sadie's father was known as Joseph Goldberg, while Jack's father was Joseph Goldstein.

[13] In writing this section, I have drawn heavily (much being quoted verbatim) from the Preface to reference[10] which is repeated as the 'Story' on the 'About' page of reference[9]. The original text was written by Esther Rosenquit (née Goldstein).

[14] POLIN Museum of the History of Polish Jews, Warsaw at https://sztetl.org.pl/en/towns/r/602-radzymin. [Accessed 16 January 2018].

[15] International Association of Jewish Genealogical Societies at http://www.iajgsjewishcemeteryproject.org/poland/radzymin-mazowieckie.html. [Accessed 16 January 2018].

[16] A *shetel* (or *sheitel*) is is a wig or half-wig worn by some orthodox Jewish married women to conform with the requirement of Jewish law to cover their heads.

[17] Also spelt[9] Yanche, sometimes known as David.

[18] As a sequel to the 1988 compilation by the children of Yosef and Feigele Goldstein "And Then There Were Eleven",[10] a second collection of memoires entitled "The Goldsteins – The Next Generation," written by the children of the original authors, and others of their generation – mainly grandchildren of Yosef's brother Yancze and his wife Choomah – was privately published as a CD in July 2001. One of the contributors, a descendant of Yosef's brother-in-law who became known as 'Mr Smith,' uses the spelling Scmideks rather than Szmidek.

[19] The first names of some of the Goldstein children are sometimes confused because of the use of Yiddish or Hebrew names (especially for the earlier born). A detailed and evidenced analysis has been carried out by my cousin, Marsha Rosenberg (daughter of Jack's youngest brother, Ron):
- **Annie** – Born in Poland. Marriage index (1927): Annie. Name on gravestone (1976): Annie (English), *Chaya* (Hebrew). It is very likely that *Chaya* was the name of Feigele's mother.
- **Lou** – Born in Poland. Marriage index (1938): Leib and Louis. Formal change of name (1947) from Leib Goldstein to Louis Grayson. Name on gravestone (1961): Louis (English), *Leibel* (Hebrew). The Goldstein family compilation "And Then There Were Eleven" [10] gives his name as Levy but there seems to be no evidence for this being his actual name. Levy and Leib sound similar but have different origins - *Levi* is Hebrew meaning a Levite and is spelled with the Hebrew letter *vav*, whereas *Leib* is Yiddish

for lion and ends with the Hebrew letter *bet*. *Leibel* is a diminutive of *Leib*. Feigele's father was Leib, so it is possible that Louis, the eldest son, will have been named after him.

- **Jack** – Born in Poland. Marriage Certificate (1934): Jacob and Jack. Hebrew name *Ya'acov*. Name on gravestone – J. Goldstein.
- **Esther** – Birth index (1914): Esther. Marriage index (1936): Esther. Name on gravestone: Esther (English), *Ester Hinda* (Hebrew).
- **Gertie** – Birth index (1916): Gertie. Marriage index (1938): Gertie. Hebrew name *Gittl*. Also known as Gert.
- **Mossy** – Birth index (1916): Morris. Marriage index (1940): Morris. Change of surname (1946-1948) from Goldstein to Gordon. Death index (2001): Morris Gordon. Name on gravestone (2001): Mossy Gordon (English), *Moshe* (Hebrew).
- **Polly** – Birth index (1918): Polly. Marriage index (1951): Pauline and Polly. Hebrew name probably *Perla*.
- **Mick** – Birth index (1920): Myer. Marriage index (1946): Michael M. Death registration (2005): Michael Myer. Name on gravestone: Mick (English), *Meir* (Hebrew). Meir was the name of Yosef's father. Curiously, Mick's birth was not registered until 1947.
- **Debbie** – Birth index (1921): Debbie. Marriage index (1941): Deborah. Death index (2005): Debbie. Name on stone Debbie (English), *Deborah* (Hebrew).
- **Ron** – Birth index (1923): Reuben. Marriage index (1949): Ronald. As a small boy he objected to being called "Ruby" as it was a girl's name, so he changed his name to Ronnie.
- **Jean** – Birth index (1929): Jean. Marriage index (1952): Jean. In the Goldstein family compilation "And Then There Were Eleven," [10] Jean is also called "Jeannie."

[20] Both Pauline and Polly are given as first names, and both Kalicstein and Kalestein are given as Wolfie's surname, in the marriage certificate.

[21] *Tzaddik* is a title in Judaism given to people considered to be righteous and saintly, such as Biblical figures and later spiritual leaders of the Hassidic community.

[22] This section is largely based on synthesis and analysis, augmented by further research and written in my own style, of the individual stories in "And Then There Were Eleven." [10]

[23] *Evening Echo*, 17 September 1991, p 4. This article comprises a slightly shortened form of an essay written by Gertie, which won first prize in a competition organised by Essex Age Concern.

[24] Boreham Street was a very short street just 1-2 small blocks north of Bethnal Green Road, near Arnold Circus in the Shoreditch area of Bethnal Green London. It ran north from Peter Street (later named Rhoda Street), in between Mount Street and Brick Lane. There was an alley at the north end into Brick Lane. It can just be seen (as 'Borham Street') in a 1922 map of the area at http://www.jewisheastend.com/Whitechapel%20map%201922.jpg. There are photographs of the houses at https://collage.cityoflondon.gov.uk/quick-search?q=boreham%20street&WINID=1516981151390.
Much of Boreham Street, including number 21, was bombed during WW2. When the site was later redeveloped, the street was no longer.
I am grateful to my cousin, Marsha Rosenberg, daughter of Ron Goldstein, for providing two side-by-side maps, (1893-1895) http://maps.nls.uk/geo/explore/side-by-side/#zoom=19&lat=51.5257&lon=-0.0724&layers=163&right=BingHyb and (1947-1964) http://maps.nls.uk/geo/explore/side-by-side/#zoom=19&lat=51.5257&lon=-0.0724&layers=173&right=BingHyb, showing the then location in relation to the present day.
[All accessed 26 January 2018].

[25] British History On-Line at http://www.british-history.ac.uk/vch/middx/vol11/pp126-132#fnn19. [Accessed 18 January 2018].

[26] A kind of mass leapfrogging, in which members of one team bent over, one behind the other, and the other team all jumped onto their backs, building up into a pyramid which eventually collapsed under pressure.

[27] Finely chopped fish, usually whitefish, pike, or carp, mixed with crumbs, chopped onion, eggs, and seasonings, cooked in a broth in the form of balls or oval-shaped cakes, and usually served chilled.

[28] A type of layered pastry, filled with apple and sultanas or other (usually) sweet filling, originating in Austria and Habsburg Empire and popular in central and eastern Europe.

[29] Now known as Rhoda Street.

[30] Tally-men and tally-women were people who sold goods on credit, especially on a door-to-door basis. They called regularly to collect the instalment payments, sometimes in a forthright manner. Interest rates could be exorbitant.

[31] *Kichlach* (singular, *kichel*) are popular Jewish biscuits commonly made with eggs, flour and sugar, rolled out flat and cut into large diamond or star shapes and baked until puffed. They are often made with a dent in the center to hold jam.

[32] A slow-cooking dish made from meat, potatoes, vegetables, beans, and rice.

[33] For a personal account, with many original photographs, see Ron Goldstein's posting in Spitalsfields Life at http://spitalfieldslife.com/2010/08/11/ron-goldstein-cambridge-bethnal-green-boys-club/#comment-1191855. [Accessed 18 January 2018].

[34] *Frum* is a Yiddish adjective meaning 'devout' or 'pious'. To be *frum* means to be committed to the observance of Jewish religious law that often exceeds the bare requirements.

[35] *Cheder* or *cheider* is a traditional school teaching the basics of Judaism and the Hebrew language. It also prepares young boys for their *bar mitzvah* and (less commonly) girls for their *bat mitzvah* [the Jewish coming-of-age ritual for boys aged 13, and girls aged 12 or 13 depending on their orthodoxy].

[36] See https://en.wikipedia.org/wiki/Eleven-plus [Accessed 7 February 2018].

[37] In the Goldstein family compilation of memories "And Then There Were Eleven,"[10] Esther called her eldest brother 'Jackie' rather than 'Jack' perhaps to avoid confusion with the person she married, Jack Rosenquit. Debbie sometimes used 'Jacky' perhaps for the same reason.

[38] 'The Love-Song of J. Alfred Prufrock' by T. S. Eliot, commonly known simply as 'Prufrock.' See, for example, http://people.virginia.edu/~sfr/enam312/prufrock.html [Accessed 12 February 2018].

[39] Sometime after Meir's death, his wife, Malke, came to London with her daughter, Ruchze [Rene], to live with her son-in-law, Smith. She died in 1935, aged 90 years, and is buried at Western Cemetery, Streatham, London.

[40] Also spelt Chuma,[9] sometimes known as Esther.

[41] Knowledge of my maternal grandparents starts with a scrap of paper left by Sadie when she passed away on 7 January 2001. It was hand-written by her father, and is as follows (spelling and grammar as in the original):
"GOLDBERG JOE   REGISTRATION No. ADOC/41/1
                 No. of Aliens Registration Cert <u>25497</u>

> This is to certify that I GOLDBERG JOE is holder of Aliens Registration Certificate No. 25497 issued at Lemon St. on 7th.2.1920 was born on 1878 in KronsKowold then occupied by Russia.
> I entered the United Kingdom on 1907, and saw service in H.M.A.F. from 2-8-1916 to 7-1-1920 in India, and from then on I have been working as a talior's machiner."

I am also indebted to my cousin, Marsha Rosenberg, daughter of Ron Goldstein, for her research and help in using this statement by my grandfather and gathering and interpreting other data used to compile this section.

[42] Końskowola is also known as *Konskovole* in Yiddish, and *Kon'skovolia* in Russian. With the onset of the Second World War, Końskowola was overrun by the German troops on 15 September, 1939. The Germans set up a prisoner of war camp and a camp for slave labour in the town. The POW camp was soon liquidated, but a labour camp continued to operate through 1943. The inmates worked for Germans-run farms, and on construction sites of roads and railroads. A Nazi ghetto was established in the town, to which many groups of Jews were relocated, including Jews expelled from Slovakia. On 8 May 1942, the Nazis conducted an *Aktion* in which many Jews were rounded up and transported to the Nazi extermination camp Sobibor. In October 1942, the ghetto's population was liquidated. In a massacre carried out by German troops, some 800-1000 Jews, among them women and children, were taken to a nearby forest and slaughtered. The ghetto's remaining inhabitants were transferred to another camp. At its height in 1914 the population of Końskowola was 5,675; in 2005 it was 2188. See https://en.wikipedia.org/wiki/Ko%C5%84skowola [Accessed 6 February 2018] and http://www.konskowola.info.pl. [Accessed 12 February 2018].

[43] Some further credence to the maiden name of Kaufman was given by my aunt Joan Goldberg (second wife of Ralph). She recalls Ralph telling her that as children the Goldberg siblings "used to go to grandma Kaufman's house and she gave us cabbage water."

[44] According to the 1901 Census, a Leah Silverman, a Spinster aged 18 (ie born 1883) was one of four boarders in the home of Mina(?) and Samuel Kaufman (a Tinplate worker) at 56 Greenfield Street, Mile End Old Town, Stepney West. She is said to have been born in 'Roumania', as were the Kaufmans. Her occupation is given as 'Tailoress'. The apparent birth year of this Leah Silverman, 1883, is a few years different to the other possible dates of 1885 and 1888, but the coincidence of the name Kaufman is striking.

[45] See http://www.25thlondon.com [accessed 24 February 2018].

[46] I am grateful to my cousin Trevor Goldberg, son of Ben and Nelly Goldberg, for a photograph of Joe's war mementoes, including his medals, and a photograph of Joe in which he is wearing them. Both photographs clearly show all three WW1 medals as described in the text.

[47] See http://www.greatwar.co.uk/medals/ww1-campaign-medals.htm#star1914 [Accessed 25 February 2018].

[48] See https://en.wikipedia.org/wiki/The_Jazz_Singer_(1980_film) [Accessed 27 February 2018].

[49] 'Prefabs' (prefabricated houses) were a major part of a plan to address the UK's housing shortage after WW2. The eventual plan was to build 300,000 units in ten years, but the programme ended after six years in 1951 with just 156,000 prefabs built. They were designed to last for ten years, but most continued inhabited for many years after that – some still in use today. See https://en.wikipedia.org/wiki/Prefabs_in_the_United_Kingdom. [Accessed 12 February 2018].

[50] Again, I have drawn heavily on the compilation of stories in "And Then There Were Eleven." [10]

[51] See the story I wrote for the BBC 'WW2 People's War' archive of World War Two memories – written by the public, gathered by the BBC at

http://www.bbc.co.uk/history/ww2peopleswar/stories/75/a8256675.shtml [Accessed 9 January 2018].

[52] 'The Traumas of Evacuation,' by Michael Goldstein, in 'Evacuees! Stories of the Children,' written by the evacuees, Edited by Terry Gasking, Twig Books, 2009; ISBN 978 09560618 05.

[53] A 'flying boat' is a fixed-winged seaplane with a hull, allowing it to land on water, and usually unable to operate on land.

[54] Gertie's autobiography, 'A Breath Of Spring' by Gertrude Denenberg, published privately by her family to celebrate her 100th birthday, in 2016.

[55] The Jewish Brigade was a military formation of the British Army composed of Jews from the settlements in Mandatory Palestine commanded by British-Jewish officers that served in Europe during WW2. It was formed in late 1944 fought the Germans in Italy.

[56] 'We Will Remember Them. A Record of the Jews Who Died in the Armed Forces of the Crown 1939-1945' by Henry Morris, Brassey's (UK) Ltd, 1989; ISBN 0-08-037705-X.

[57] See, for example, https://kenfentonswar.com/raf-training. [Accessed 3 March 2018].

[58] See http://www.abct.org.uk/airfields/airfield-finder/evanton-novar. [Accessed 3 March 2018].

[59] 'Temporary' referred to the fact Jack was holding a substantive post on a wartime Temporary Establishment. It did not mean he was a substantive Cpl/LAC, as this would have been shown as Acting rather than Temporary. All promotions and appointments in the armed forces during the WW2 period were officially of a temporary nature only and would have no standing once the period of hostilities was over. Generally, the 'Temporary' prefix was omitted in most references to an individual but might be included in some formal references such as on a record of service form. See

http://www.rafcommands.com/forum/showthread.php?18081-T-Sgt. [Accessed 3 March 2018].

[60] The Royal Air Force introduced heavy conversion units (HCU) in late 1941 to qualify crews trained on medium bombers to operate heavy (four-engine) bombers such as Lancasters before final posting to the operational squadrons. Some of the HCUs were involved in bombing operations over Germany. See https://en.wikipedia.org/wiki/List_of_Royal_Air_Force_conversion_units. [Accessed 25 March 2018]

[61] Royal Canadian Air Force. Great numbers of Canadians served in units of the Royal Air Force, and by the time of the German surrender, 48 RCAF squadrons were overseas, virtually completely manned by Canadian officers and men. A landmark was the formation of No. 6 (RCAF) Bomber Group of Bomber Command on 1 January 1943; it grew ultimately to 14 squadrons. In Bomber Command alone, 9919 Canadians lost their lives.[62] Canadian airmen served in every theatre, from bases in the UK, North Africa, Italy, northwest Europe and southeast Asia. Squadrons in North America worked in antisubmarine operations off the Atlantic coast and co-operated with US air forces against the Japanese in the Aleutian Islands. At one time or another seven RCAF squadrons served in the RAF's Coastal Command over the Atlantic. RCAF aircraft destroyed or had a part in destroying 20 enemy submarines. In the northwest Europe campaign of 1944–45, the RCAF deployed 17 squadrons. During the war 232,632 men and 17,030 women served in the RCAF, and 17,101 lost their lives. See http://www.thecanadianencyclopedia.ca/en/article/second-world-war-wwii. [Accessed 1 April 2018].

[62] 'The Bomber Command War Diaries. An Operational Reference Book 1939-1945' by Martin Middlebrook and Chris Everitt, Midland Publishing, Revised Paperback Edition, 1996; ISBN 1 85780 033 8. This is a remarkably complete record of every operation of Bomber Command during WW2, set out day-by-day with details of the raids and impacts.

[63] Bomber Command was organised into Groups, each comprising up to 18 Squadrons, each having 20-30 aircraft. Jack's 166 Squadron was in Group 1. It initially operated Wellington bombers but these were replaced by Lancasters in September 1943.[64] In all it carried out 245 bombing raids and 46 minelaying raids. There were 5068 sorties, losing 153 aircraft; 22 others were destroyed in crashes.[62] The Squadron was disbanded on 18 November 1945.[64]

[64] 'Avro Lancaster the Definitive Record' by Harry Holmes, Airlife Publishing Ltd, second Edition 2001; ISBN 1 84037 288 5. This is an astonishingly full and detailed record of the history of each and every Lancaster aircraft – their manufacture, deployment, operations, service, and losses.

[65] The outline of this record was initially compiled by my uncle Ron Goldstein, Jack's youngest brother, as part of his research over the period November 1995 to August 1997. As Jack's log book is missing, the record was taken from a copy of the log book of the Flight Engineer, Ted Hull, which (according to Ted) would be almost identical to Jack's. The record Ron compiled has been augmented here by information from other sources. [67] [68] [66] [67] [68] The 5 March raid on Chemnitz was not included in Ron Goldstein's summary. This is somewhat surprising, since the raid was a continuation of 'Operation Thunderclap' (earlier phases on 13 and 14 February 1945 to Dresden and Chemnitz respectively), and the number of aircraft participating from 166 Squadron was actually greater at 26 (cf 24-25 earlier), probably all or virtually all the Lancasters available; moreover, RF154 is specifically mentioned elsewhere as participating in this raid.[66] Jack is therefore considered to have participated in the 5 March raid on Chemnitz.

[66] For full details of all the raids by 166 Squadron between 1 February 1945 and 16 March 1945, see 'Wings of War: History of 166 Squadron' by Jim Wright, 166 Squadron Association, 1996; ISBN-13 978-0952847601.

[67] Some details on raids in February 1945 have been taken from http://webarchive.nationalarchives.gov.uk/20070706055854/http://

www.raf.mod.uk/bombercommand/feb45.html. [Accessed 5 March 2018].

[68] Some details on raids in March 1945 have been taken from http://webarchive.nationalarchives.gov.uk/20070706060012/http://www.raf.mod.uk/bombercommand/mar45.html. [Accessed 5March 2018].

[69] This became the regular aircraft of Jack's crew. It was nicknamed 'TARFU' – 'Things are Really F***ed Up.'

[70] In a letter to my uncle Ron Goldstein dated 21 January 1996, Alf White claimed that the incendiaries had fallen onto AS-B from another Lancaster above them on the raid.

[71] This is likely to have been an error – there seem to have been 16 operational flights of Jack's crew.[65]

[72] The nick-name 'Chuck' and 'Chock' seem both to have been used.

[73] The Lancasters were each powered by four Rolls Royce Merlin engines.

[74] The 4000lb high capacity bomb was the first of the large blast bombs to be designed, and at the time was the largest ever to have been dropped by the British Air Force. See http://www.wwiiequipment.com/index.php?option=com_content&view=article&id=107:4000lb-high-capacity-bomb&catid=43:bombs&Itemid=60. [Accessed 6 March 2018].

[75] There were six 1000lb incendiary clusters on board.

[76] The rest of the crew appear not to have noticed this, although Lefty reported trouble later in the flight.

[77] These were half-hourly wind forecasts based on information radioed back to England by selected Pathfinder Aircraft. These

were primarily target-marking squadrons whose function was to locate and mark targets with flares, which a main bomber force could aim at, increasing the accuracy of their bombing. See https://en.wikipedia.org/wiki/Pathfinder_%28RAF%29. [Accessed 6 March 2018].

[78] H2S was the first airborne, ground scanning radar system. It was developed for the Royal Air Force's Bomber Command during World War II to identify targets on the ground for night and all-weather bombing. This allowed attacks outside the range of the various radio navigation aids, which were limited to about 350 kilometres (220 miles). It was also widely used as a general navigation system, allowing landmarks to be identified at long range. See https://en.wikipedia.org/wiki/H2S_%28radar%29. [Accessed 6 March 2018].

[79] This timing is of significance when compared with the Luftwaffe claims report of that evening, in which a *Feldwebel* [Sergeant] Shuster claims to have shot down a Lancaster bomber at 9.31 over North Nürnberg.

[80] This was a welterweight boxing match between RAF Sergeant Ernie Roderick and Sergeant Arthur Danahar of the Irish Guards, for the Welterweight championship of Great Britain, at the Royal Albert Hall, in aid of the RAF Benevolent Fund. Roderick won, and the RAF Benevolent Fund benefited by nearly £6000. See http://www.tcd.ie/irishfilm/print.php?search=keyword&q=boxing&exactMatch=. [Accessed 6 March 2018].

[81] These were coloured flares which hung in the sky for some time and so were effective in target-marking. The name derives from Wanganui, one of the earliest cities in New Zealand to adopt the custom of lighting a Christmas Tree with electric lights in a park near the city centre. Many New Zealanders served as crew in Bomber Command, and it was they who called the marker flares 'Wanganui flares' instead of the more usual name 'Christmas tree flares' used by master bombers and pathfinder aircraft. See

http://www.ww2incolor.com/forum/showthread.php/11622-Wanganui-flares-(Bomber-comand). [Accessed 6 March 2018].

[82] An astrodome is a hemispherical transparent dome fitted in the cabin roof of an aircraft to allow the use of a sextant during astro-navigation. See https://en.wikipedia.org/wiki/Astrodome_(aeronautics). [Accessed 6 March 2018].

[83] In a telephone conversation with Ron Goldstein on 1 February 1996, Alf White said he was convinced that Jack never had the chance to bail out. But during a four-hour meeting with Ron at Alf's home in Luton on 24 April 1997, Alf said: "When I tapped [Jack] on the knee he was already three-quarters out of his turret and he was standing on the step which he would have used to get out of the turret." He could not recall having previously said that Jack "never had the chance to bail out." It is however clear from all the post-crash evidence, that Jack did not get out of the turret. Alf also told Ron that his nephew, Anthony Cutler, had made contact with a farmer near the crash site, who claimed there was no-one in the aircraft when it crash-landed; this is unsubstantiated and contrary to all other evidence.

[84] This would indicate that someone had previously bailed out from this hatch.

[85] Supplied to Ron Goldstein by Mark Charnley, 166 Squadron Historian.

[86] 'Nachtjagd War Diaries Vol 2. An Operational History of the German Night Fighter Force in the West, April 1944 - May 1945' by Dr Theo Boiten, Red Kite, 2008; ISBN-13 978-1906592004. I am grateful to Kelvin Youngs of the Aircrew Remembrance Society for referring me to this publication.

[87] See http://www.luftwaffe39-45.historia.nom.br/ases/vitorias_lutje.htm. [Accessed 25 March 2018].

[88] The Geneva Convention (1929) was signed at Geneva on 27 July 1929. Its official name is the 'Convention relative to the Treatment of Prisoners of War, Geneva July 27, 1929.' It entered into force on 19 June 1931. It is this version of the Geneva Conventions which covered the treatment of prisoners of war during WW2. See https://en.wikipedia.org/wiki/Geneva_Convention_(1929). [Accessed 11 March 2018].

[89] According to Jack's Service Record, he was only 5ft 2¼in on entry to the RAF.

[90] Jim MacDonald, founder member of The Wickenby Register (The 12 & 626 Squadron Association), told Ron (telephone conversation on 1 May 1997) that "it was common knowledge in the RAF that [captured] crew were being killed by the Germans…. Jack would have been a brave man to have flown under the name of Goldstein."

[91] Sadly, Ted passed away in June 2001, and Betty, his wife, in July 2011.

[92] This was in fact the Bomb Aimer of Lancaster PD275, Sergeant JH ('Jim') Clarke, RCAF.

[93] Gertie was a frequent writer of articles and poetry and had much published.

[94] It was the last heavy Bomber Command raid over Nürnberg, but not the last air raid over Germany.[62]

[95] It is not at all clear where this suggestion came from originally. I recall as a child thinking this was how Jack died, and believe Sadie thought that too (perhaps she told me?). In Sadie's letter to Lou dated 19 June 1945, given earlier, having just visited the War Office, she says: "according to the P/O and W.O.P. Jack was killed by German ack-ack ground fire while baling out." It is unclear who/what are the 'P/O' and the 'W.O.P.' but as Sadie's visit to the

War Office was before the report of the Missing Search and Enquiry Unit (6 December 1946), the information would have been premature and unreliable. Ted Hull thought[7] that Sadie had been told that Jack 'was killed whilst baling out.' Another suggestion, based on reports of the crews of other aircraft on the Nürnberg raid, was that the aircraft exploded before hitting the ground, but that is also not true. It is unequivocal, as the evidence in this book demonstrates, that Jack crashed still in the aircraft.

[96] *Kaddish* is a liturgical prayer recited by mourners after the death of a close relative. See http://www.dictionary.com/browse/kaddish. [Accessed 12 March 2018].

[97] Star of David.

[98] The circumstances of families bereaved by husbands being killed in WW2, and the issues surrounding the pensions awarded to them, are vividly described in 'War's Forgotten Women – British Widows of the Second World War' by Maureen Shaw and Helen D Millgate, The History Press, 2011; ISBN 978 0 7524 6179 3.

[99] See http://www.nordbayern.de/region/schwabach/verheerender-abschuss-1.2771997. [Accessed 25 March 2018].

[100] See https://www.webarchive.org.uk/wayback/archive/20121121082538/http://www.aircrewremembrancesociety.com/raf1945/3/daymondkeith.html. [Accessed 15 March 2018].

[101] See http://raf166squadron.com/RollofHonour07.htm. [Accessed 27 March 2018].

[102] See https://www.cwgc.org/find-a-cemetery/cemetery/2008700/DURNBACH%20WAR%20CEMETERY. [Accessed 1 April 2018].

[103] *El Maleh Rahamim* (God full of compassion) is a prayer for the soul of departed that is recited with a haunting chant at funeral

services or on visiting the graves of relatives. See https://www.myjewishlearning.com/article/el-maleh-rahamim. [Accessed 16 March 2018].

[104] See https://reformjudaism.org/practice/ask-rabbi/why-do-jews-put-small-stones-tombstones-when-visiting-cemetery-0. [Accessed 16 March 2018].

[105] See http://www.tempsford.20m.com/v9976.html. [Accessed 17 March 2018].

[106] Excerpts from all Lynn Alleway's films can be seen on her website http://www.lynnalleway.com. [Accessed 17 March 2018]. Examples are:
- 'The Conman, his Lover and the Prime Minister's Wife,' about Carole Caplin, who was embroiled in a tabloid scandal because of her relationship with the then Prime Minister's wife, Cherie Blair;
- 'Tough Kids - Tough Love,' about the care of vulnerable children and young people by Camila Batmanghelidjh, founder of the charity Kids Company – I am in no doubt that this TV film helped enormously in gaining government money and in due course Camila raising around £18 million a year herself;
- 'Holloway: the young Ones,' involving spending three months inside Holloway women's prison;
- 'Baby Hospital,' the stories of couples' experiences of losing a child and the role of the neonatal intensive care unit at Liverpool Women's Hospital;
- A series of three documentaries about the Amish, the Hutterites, and the Mormons;
- Documentaries on Mr and Mrs Bin Laden, Gareth Gates, and Kerry Katona.

[107] As a parting gift, Melanie gave me some packets of Klösse, and after I returned home she sent me recipes for both this and Sauerbraten. See https://www.allrecipes.com/recipe/221361/traditional-sauerbraten,

https://allrecipes.com/recipe/61002/kartoffel-kloesse-potato-dumplings, and http://www.gomeal.de/uploaded_img/Kndel-und-Kle.jpg. [All accessed 17 March 2018].

[108] Hans Muschweck, Melanie's maternal grandfather, was born 18 July 1932 in Kammerstein. His father left his mother before he was born, so he never knew his father. To make matters worse, his mother died a few days after his birth. As a result, he lived mostly with his grandfather who had also been widowed, as well as with various of his mother's siblings, so it was great coincidence was that he was in Kammerstein at the time of Jack's crash. When he wrote his statement for me he was in poor physical health, but his mind was sound and very clear.

[109] The RAF 166 Squadron website at http://raf166squadron.com/RF154%20AS-B.htm, with photographs at http://raf166squadron.com/SurvivedChurchward.htm. [Both accessed 27 March 2018].

[110] The 'Back to Normandy' website at https://www.backtonormandy.org/component/mtree/air-force-operations/airplanes-allies-and-axis-lost/lancaster/20871-RF1541945-03-17.html. [Accessed 27 March 2018].

[111] 'Royal Air Force Bomber Command Losses of the Second World War, Vol 6, Aircraft and Crew Losses 1945' by W R Chorley, Midland Counties Publications, 1998; ISBN 0 904597 92 X.

[112] 'Royal Air Force Bomber Command Losses of the Second World War, Vol 9, Roll of Honour 1939-1945' by W R Chorley, Midland Publishing, 2007; ISBN (13) 978 1 85780 195 8.

[113] See http://internationalbcc.co.uk. [Accessed 29 March 2018].

[114] See http://www.thenma.org.uk. [Accessed 29 March 2018].

[115] There is uncertainty as to the birth year, as explained in the text.

CPSIA information can be obtained
at www.ICGtesting.com
Printed in the USA
LVHW072131220722
724231LV00019B/379